# The *The* **Cup** *and the* **Glory**

# Study Guide

### Lessons on
### Suffering and
### the Glory of God

## GREG HARRIS

**Kress Christian**
PUBLICATIONS

*The Cup and the Glory Study Guide*

© 2008 Greg Harris

Published by:

## Kress Christian
### PUBLICATIONS

P.O. Box 132228
The Woodlands, TX 77393
www.kresschristianpublications.com

Unless otherwise indicated, all Scripture quotations were taken from the NEW
AMERICAN STANDARD BIBLE ®, Copyright © 1960, 1962, 1963, 1968, 1971, 1972,
1973, 1975, 1977 by the Lockman foundation. Used by Permission.

ISBN 1-934952-00-1

Editorial Consultants: Kevin McAteer, Rebecca R. Howard
Cover Design: Layne Moore, Layne Moore Group
Text Design: Valerie Moreno

Significant contributions made (written, verbally, or both) in order of appearance: Chris E. Bush,
Bradley P. Sewell, Paula Adams, Jeff Terrell, Jonathan Szeto, Eric Swanson, David Lee, Jared
Beaird, Matt McGuillicuddy, Jody Faison, Peter Barber, Leland White, my two prayer classes at
The Master's Seminary (Spring 2007), Betsy Harris, and lastly, as one untimely born and grafted
in: Johnny McClaughlin.

# Contents

Introduction: How to Use the Study Guide 5

Chapter 1      The Wilderness      7

Chapter 2      The Cup      11

Chapter 3      The Road      17

Chapter 4      The Gift      23

Chapter 5      The Fellowship      29

Chapter 6      The Footprints      35

Chapter 7      The Surprise      41

Chapter 8      The Blessing      47

Chapter 9      The Agreement      53

Chapter 10      The Glory      59

End of Study: Summary Questions 65

Q & A: Interview with Betsy Harris 67

The Writing of The Cup and the Glory 71

# *Introduction*

# *How to Use the Study Guide*

The study guide is designed for use by individuals or for use by small groups. In my travel and correspondence I have noticed the wide variety that exists of good (or bad) commentaries available to people. In several places around the world Christians have only their Bible and nothing else. Several others have one to three Christian books. Some have rather large personal libraries and electronic media available to them.

So how do I set up a study guide for those with such a vast discrepancy in what is available to them? I have tried to make this study to be "Word driven," that is, from the Scriptures so that with the help of the book, people will be able to follow along. *The Cup and the Glory (www.glorybooksministry.org)* is only as good as it is biblically accurate. If there is any comfort and encouragement, it is because God uses His Word. I use *The Cup and the Glory* as one of the textbooks in the prayer class that I teach at The Master's Seminary, but truthfully, the only one sure text we have is the Word of God.

Even though I use the book as a textbook, I rarely read from it in class; instead we focus more on the biblical texts that were referenced in the book. The same will be true for this study guide. It is not so much trying to bring out gold nuggets from the book, but rather that the book will point to gold nuggets in the Word.

For those who do not have any other sources available, *The MacArthur Study Bible* would be the one resource I recommend as a beginning point. Obviously, if you have access to them, The *MacArthur Commentary Series* would contain much more material.

The format of the study guide for each chapter is as follows:

1. **Scripture References:** These refer to the broader context that you can read to get the flow of the Bible verses. The specific references will be given also.

2. **Reading Assignments:** These will generally be the assignments from *The Cup and the Glory*. This is a reminder that the questions should be considered after reading the chapters or the entire book. In fact, many of the questions will make no sense unless one has read the chapters.

3. **Questions from *The Cup and the Glory*:** These will be given with page numbers, which will be useful in either reviewing or contemplating important points.

4. **Questions from the Word:** These will be primarily from the highlighted text with some of the other Scripture passages cited.

5. **The Heart of the Matter:** These will pinpoint the significance or "make sure you understand this" points of the chapter. If you missed these, you may go back to the previous sections and find the answers.

6. **Personal Application Section:** This is to be used first for yourself and then in ministering to others. As you will see, this will be set up with many of your own interactions with God and His Word.

7. **Deeper Walk Study:** This section takes a little longer. No classes, message series, or books can ever deplete the supply of gold nuggets in God's Word. This section is for those who want to follow the "where do I go from here" for additional biblical truths that one can research. As before, this is set up primarily so that one can do this entirely from the Bible. Of course, any good, solid commentary will enhance your study.

*Just a quick note:* I did not select any daily reading section for the study guide. I realize that *The Cup and the Glory* is meat—not milk. I have heard from many people who tell me that they have to stop and read a sentence, paragraph, page or chapter over and over and meditate on it. Sometimes it is a matter of conviction that God is doing in their lives as Christians. I do not want to hinder any such work of the Spirit. I would rather God do the timing. For those who want to do daily reading, you may divide the material according to your own pace.

I very much hope this will be a fruitful study unto the Glory of God.

To God be the Glory!

Greg Harris
July 2007
The Master's Seminary

P.S. Oh, yes, I almost forgot; I didn't mention my "price" for this study guide. There is no profit for me in writing this work; even the printed edition is done virtually at cost. My price is that you will please pray for me and pass the book and the study guide on to someone you think would benefit from them. It is a ministry, not a business.

# Chapter One

# The Wilderness

Because most of "The Wilderness" is my personal testimony, this chapter differs from the others. This chapter contains more personal references and much less Scripture than the rest of the book; however, there are still matters to consider.

## SCRIPTURE REFERENCES

Key passages used in this chapter include: 1 Thessalonians 4:13-18; Colossians 2:1; 1 Peter 5:10.

## READING ASSIGNMENTS

Read chapter one "The Wilderness" before attempting to answer any of the following questions.

## QUESTIONS FROM *THE CUP AND THE GLORY*

1. According to the book, how does the author define "the wilderness" (pp. 14-15)?

   _____

   _____

   _____

   _____

2. How did the wilderness change his prayer life (pp. 15-17)? Why?

   _____

   _____

   _____

   _____

3. Why was 1 Peter 5:10 so difficult for Greg Harris to read? Why did he not want to preach this passage when he was asked (p. 18)?

   _____

   _____

   _____

   _____

## QUESTIONS FROM THE WORD

1.  Why would Paul end 1 Thessalonians 4 with the command to "comfort one another with these words?" What comfort did God intend for the Thessalonians? How is this comforting?

    _____

    _____

    _____

    _____

2.  What can we learn about Paul and his prayer life in Colossians 2:1 (p. 15)? How does this broaden your understanding of how difficult prayer can be? Explain.

    _____

    _____

    _____

    _____

3.  First Peter 5:10 will be an important verse in the study and will be examined in an upcoming chapter. What are some of the biblical truths taken from this verse? List Who promises, what He promises and when He promises them.

    _____

    _____

    _____

    _____

## THE HEART OF THE MATTER

Even though this is a different chapter from the others, there are still central points to identify. Remember, this section is primarily for review to ensure that you thoroughly understand these points:

1.  Having defined the wilderness as "that baffling condition of going from spiritual light into spiritual darkness" (pp. 14-15), it is crucial that one is walking with God when this condition occurs. How does someone in this situation differ from those who have the ramifications of some specific sin they had committed (such as the sin of David and Bathsheba in 2 Samuel 11)? Explain.

    _____

    _____

    _____

    _____

3. The "Prosperity Gospel" teaches that God wants you to be healthy, wealthy and happy; and if you are not, then it is due to some sin in your life. Explain how the testimony and the Scripture dispute this?

_____

_____

_____

_____

## PERSONAL APPLICATION SECTION

1. Was the 1 Thessalonians 4:13-18 passage appropriate to end the twins' letter? Why or why not (p. 11)?

_____

_____

_____

_____

2. When would it be appropriate to use the passage to comfort someone? When would it be inappropriate? Explain.

_____

_____

_____

_____

3. Write your own personal application question from this chapter (in other words, "what have I learned") that was not asked elsewhere and give the answer to your question.

_____

_____

_____

_____

## DEEPER WALK STUDY

For those who want to research additional related Scripture and topics, consider the following:

1. How does the Book of Numbers being entitled "In the Wilderness" in the Hebrew text change your understanding of what the book teaches? Explain.

_____

_____

_____

_____

2.  Read the book of Numbers, or at least start with Numbers chapter 9, and trace the people's re-
    peated disobedience and the judgments of God. Pay careful attention to chapters 13–14 because
    their rebellion had severe consequences for them.

    _____

    _____

    _____

    _____

3.  Notice the difference between God leading someone into the wilderness who is walking with
    God (p. 17) versus the nation of Israel being in the wilderness as consequences of their own sin-
    fulness and rebellion. What are the similarities between the two conditions? What are the diff-
    erences? Explain.

    _____

    _____

    _____

    _____

# Chapter Two

# The Cup

## SCRIPTURE REFERENCES

Key passages used in this chapter include: Mark 9–10 (broader text); Matthew 16–19 (parallel text); Mark 9:1-10; 10:35-41 (specific text).

## READING ASSIGNMENTS

Read chapter two "The Cup" before attempting to answer any of the following questions.

## QUESTIONS FROM *THE CUP AND THE GLORY*

1. Although James and John are often criticized regarding their request of Jesus, what are some of the other important matters to consider about what they had asked (pp. 20-22)? Explain the significance.

_____

_____

_____

_____

2. What did the rich young ruler seek from Jesus? How did Jesus' answer demonstrate that the man had by no means kept all the commandments all his life (pp. 25-27)?

_____

_____

_____

_____

3. How does the apostles' astonishment at what Jesus taught regarding riches show how they defined being blessed by God (pp. 27-28)?

_____

_____

_____

_____

4. Based on what had already happened and what Jesus had already taught, why was the request of James and John a logical one (pp. 29-31)?

_____

_____

_____

_____

5. Jesus asked if James and John were able to drink the cup. What are some of the possible elements of drinking the cup (pp. 33-35)?

_____

_____

_____

_____

ou will find, however, suffering changes the scope of your prayer life. It causes you to reexamine the content of what you ask, especially when contrasted with the pleasant junctures of your Christian walk. This does not mean you are wrong in asking God for things, but you will find suffering cultivates a different mentality regarding what you ask. Your prayers are not the same when you are looking up from the pit. In fact, an aspect of suffering occurs when God does not grant many of the requests we bring to Him, at least not in a way we expect or even appreciate. Intense and prolonged suffering forces you to address in your own life the simple yet profound questions, "What do you want from Jesus? What do you want from God?" The questions are not as easy as they sound—and the answer is even more difficult. If you pray for a deeper walk with Jesus or deeper blessings in the spiritual realm—and really mean it—how God answers these prayers precious to Him may surprise you. It will most assuredly stretch your faith. Answered prayers of a deeper walk or deeper blessings are not so much a matter of God giving these to us as much as it is for Him to bring us to the point where we can receive them. The road to spiritual deepness with God is unexpectedly long and often severe with its numerous pitfalls and impediments. Once we grasp this concept, it will make us consider the cost before we ask God to have His own way with us.

—*The Cup and the Glory*, pp. 19-20

## QUESTIONS FROM THE WORD

1. How does Mark 9:1 set the stage for the Transfiguration? How does Mark 9:2-8 set the stage for what will ultimately be asked by James and John in Mark 10:35-41 (pp. 22-24)?

_____

_____

_____

_____

2. Based on 2 Peter 1:16-18 and John 1:14, why did Mark 9:1-8 so greatly affect Peter, James and John (pp. 23-24)?

_____

_____

_____

_____

3. With all that had taken place, how would Jesus' answer to Peter be understood by him in Matthew 19:27-28 (pp. 28-29)? (Remember that the Transfiguration already had occurred in Matthew 17/Mark 9/Luke 9.) What does Luke 19:11 teach regarding the expectation of the apostles (p.29)? How would that affect their understanding of upcoming events?

_____

_____

_____

_____

4. What is the significance of the six uses of the Greek word *de* ("but") in Mark 10:35-41 (pp. 32-33)?

_____

_____

_____

_____

*J*esus' response to James and John's request casts a piercing light on our own hearts and our own understanding, or stated better, our own misunderstanding of prayer. For instance, Jesus told James and John they did not "know" what they asked, using a Greek word meaning, "to know intellectually; to understand." Scripture does not give any record of the facial expressions of James and John but they must have looked incredulous after the reply of Jesus. To them, it must have seemed at the time as though Jesus did not understand them. James and John "knew" what they wanted—and they knew He knew—and made request for it, being not at all ambiguous in what they asked. What they did not understand was the nature of prayer. They looked at their request as totally contingent on Jesus. He has what they wanted, He could open His "gift bag," wave His hand, and give it to them, much as He had done with the turning of the water into wine and the feeding of the multitudes. What they failed to see at this point in their spiritual life was that it was not so much contingent on the ability of the One to give it as it was on their spiritual capacity to receive it. God is more than willing and gracious to give them—and us—what we pray for to the extent it accomplishes His own glory and our own ultimate good. The question is whether we are willing to let God bring us to the point where we are vessels fit to receive the deeper blessings from Him. So instead of "Give me this, Lord," our prayer should be "Lord, please work in my life and remove the obstacles that keep me from knowing You better and which keep Me from being the vessel prepared for a deeper walk, deeper service and deeper blessings."

—*The Cup and the Glory*, p. 31

## THE HEART OF THE MATTER

If you are unable to answer the following questions biblically, study the appropriate sections again.

1.  Why would James and John be surprised at the way Jesus answered them in Mark 9-10?

    _____

    _____

    _____

    _____

2.  Why did Jesus answer James and John in the way that He did? What needed to take place in order for Him to answer their prayers (pp.31-32)?

    _____

    _____

    _____

    _____

3.  Why didn't James and John really know what they were asking Jesus in Mark 10:35-41 (pp. 30-32)?

    _____

    _____

    _____

    _____

4.  What is the difference and the significance of the active voice ("drinking the cup") versus the passive voice ("to be baptized")? Name some examples of each (pp. 33-35).

    _____

    _____

_____

_____

e can learn another lesson from this one encounter with Jesus. In receiving the deeper blessings of God, we have a part and God has a part. Jesus asked James and John if they were "able," from the Greek word *dynamai*, which means "to be able," or "to have the power." It is where we get our English word "dynamite." Were they able to drink the cup He drinks or to be baptized with the baptism with which He was baptized? Jesus employed two metaphors in His questioning response, one active and one passive. In drinking the cup we do the action (active); we willfully partake of it. In being baptized we receive the action (passive); we submit to what God gives us. One is a voluntary choice on our part—which by no means is easy—and the other is to respond by faith to the cross we bear in whatever God brings or allows into our lives, to count the cost, and keep going on in faith.

*—The Cup and the Glory*, p. 33

## PERSONAL APPLICATION SECTION

1. Why is the repeated phrase written with an ellipsis (i.e., "the three dots"): "By the way, what do you pray for . . . when you pray?" What do you think?

_____

_____

_____

_____

2. How similar is the request made by James and John to your own request of "Jesus, I want You to do whatever I ask?" In what way are they the same? In what way do they differ? Explain.

_____

_____

_____

_____

3. Would you be as astonished by the answer Jesus gave after the rich young ruler left as the immediate disciples were? Does your prayer life give proof of that (pp. 27-28)?

_____

_____

_____

_____

4. What do you pray for . . . when you pray?

_____

_____

_____

_____

5. Write your own personal application question from this chapter (in other words, "what have I learned") that was not asked elsewhere and give the answer to your question.

_____

_____

_____

_____

> *W*e should also realize that we do not "know" ("to understand") what we ask any more than James and John did. A refining process occurs that makes us fit to receive the deeper blessings of God. Yet our prayers focus mostly on the removal of the very elements God uses to bring us to the point of blessing. Is it any wonder Paul would say, "We do not know ["understand"] how to pray as we should" in Romans 8:26? We pray for greatness and blessing from God, and then for relief from the divine procedure that accomplishes this. On top of that, we usually blame God for unanswered prayers, while all the time He is in the process of answering what we glibly bring before Him.
>
> —*The Cup and the Glory*, p. 35

## DEEPER WALK STUDY

For those who want to research additional related Scripture and topics, consider the following:

Almost a year transpired between Mark 9 and Mark 10, especially Mark 10:35-41 (p. 24). Trace and write what else Jesus did and said in the chapters that give additional information during this time, namely Luke 10–13 and John 7–10. This will give a better understanding of what Peter, James and John had heard. Remember, other than Jesus, no one knows of His glory like they do.

# Chapter Three

# The Road

## SCRIPTURE REFERENCES

Key passages used in this book include: Psalm 143; 2 Corinthians 4:8; 11:26-17; 12:1-6; especially Acts 16:1-10.

## READING ASSIGNMENTS

Read chapter three "The Road" before attempting to answer any of the following questions.

## QUESTIONS FROM *THE CUP AND THE GLORY*

1. God took Paul from times of blessing into times of darkness. Give examples of how God did this (pp. 39-41). Why would God do this?

   _____

   _____

   _____

   _____

2. Paul walked both a physical and a spiritual road to Troas. What are some of the elements that may be true for others on their own "road to Troas" (pp. 43-44)?

   _____

   _____

   _____

   _____

3. Where should we begin before questioning God regarding an area of perplexity in our lives (p. 44)?

   _____

   _____

   _____

   _____

4. How did Paul's walk differ from those in John 6:66 (p. 45)? Explain.

_____

_____

_____

_____

5. How can a "no" from God actually be an indication of what His will is (pp. 45-46)?

_____

_____

_____

_____

6. What should be the primary goal of the believer (pp. 46-47)? What hinders this goal?

_____

_____

_____

_____

7. God repeatedly closed doors for Paul on the road to Troas. Name one blessing that he received as a result (p. 48).

_____

_____

_____

_____

However, perplexity can lead to a worse condition. Perplexity expanded results in despair. In the Greek there is a play on words. Despair is *exaporeo*, from the same root word as "perplexed" (*aporeo*), but in an intensified form that is difficult to carry over into English. If perplexity means, "no way out," then despair means, "NO WAY OUT!" Despair is a much deeper pit than perplexity. Despair results not only when circumstances completely baffle us, but also when one is entirely devoid of hope. Paul wrote that he was not at that point yet—but many of us have been, and many of us still are. If you are, you are far from the first believer to despair before God. Many personalities of the Bible, as well as through the long history of those who walk closely with God, have descended into the temporary hopelessness that accompanies despair. However, while despairing is common with many, it is not unavoidable.

—*The Cup and the Glory*, pp. 39-40

# QUESTIONS FROM THE WORD

1.  From the Greek word studies, what do the words "perplexity" and "despair" mean (p. 39)? How are these words similar? How are they different?

    _____

    _____

    _____

    _____

2.  List the multiple blessings that God gave Paul during Acts 16:1-5 (pp. 40-41).

    _____

    _____

    _____

    _____

3.  How does Acts 16:6-10 show the sovereignty of God? List examples and explain. If you want to continue this question, how does the episode with Lydia and the ladies by the riverside (Acts 16: 13-14) and the Philippian jailer (16:22-34) give further evidence of God's sovereignty? Explain.

    _____

    _____

    _____

    _____

4.  Why would Acts 16 include a reference to each member of the Trinity (p. 46)?

    _____

    _____

    _____

    _____

5.  How do all the requirements of the walk to Troas (Acts 16:1-10; pp. 44-46) harmonize with Proverbs 3:5-6 (p. 47)? How did Paul's walk model these verses? Explain.

    _____

    _____

    _____

    _____

> o Paul and his few companions walk, and they do not know where they are going. They
> walk, and every effort they attempt—even good and noble endeavors as part of their fulfill-
> ment of their call to the ministry—comes to an unexpected and unexplained halt. So they continue
> to walk, 500 miles from Lystra to Troas, not seeing the active hand of God's blessing in their lives.
> During the journey of Acts 16:5-10 there is no report of "success," no visible fruit, no churches
> planted, no lives changed by the Gospel, no seeing the powerful hand of the Lord operative as He
> had displayed just weeks previously. Probably as perplexing as anything, God disclosed no divine
> direction in the sense of where they should go or how long they should walk.
>
> —*The Cup and the Glory*, p. 42

## THE HEART OF THE MATTER

By way of review, make sure that you are able to answer biblically the following questions. If you are not, go back and study again the appropriate sections.

There are five requirements which must be in place if one is going to walk on the road to Troas with God and before one can question God about matters of perplexity. Make sure that you know these. Write them.

(p. 44) _____

(pp. 44-45) _____

(p. 45) _____

(pp. 45-46) _____

(pp. 46-47) _____

## PERSONAL APPLICATION SECTION

1.  How does this chapter change your understanding of God and His ways during your own time of extended perplexity? Explain.

    _____

    _____

    _____

    _____

2.  Explain some of the hindrances which keep us from walking on the road that God has for us.

    _____

    _____

_____

_____

3. Were you convicted or encouraged (or both) by Lauren's questions on the trip to the wedding (p. 49)? Why?

_____

_____

_____

_____

4. Are there some areas in which you are not fully trusting God or have not fully surrendered to God's care? What are these areas? From what you have learned, what are you going to do about them? Write these (with the date when you intend to take action). You may need to come back to this as a reminder.

_____

_____

_____

_____

5. Write your own personal application question from this chapter (in other words, "what have I learned") that was not asked elsewhere and give the answer to your question.

_____

_____

_____

_____

It is not easy walking on the road to Troas. You do not understand what God is doing in your own life. You do not understand how the personal blessings and visible fruit of Acts 16:5 turn into the wilderness journey of 16:6-8. When others ask you, "How are you doing?" or "What are you doing?," it sounds so ridiculously naïve to say, "I don't know."

It's not fun walking to Troas, to be in a situation where it seems as though God's blessing is something in the past for you, as it appears He has turned His smile to someone else. When you're walking on the road to Troas, you cannot even give yourself away. Everything you try to do—even good endeavors with good motives—receives a divine prohibition. The only answer you get is, "Keep walking," and even that answer being derived only because you have no alternative other than to give up on God.

It can be quite lonely while walking to Troas. You will find fewer and fewer people with you the farther along you walk. Multiple exits of escape tempt and allure along the way, and many take advantage of this avenue of departure from the road to Troas. Still the road remains, and the Lord beckons us to follow.

Two related items the road to Troas will reveal to you: the degree you really trust God, and the degree that you are pliable in His hand. Do you trust God only when He gives you our heart's delight, or can you trust Him when He does not? You will learn all about this—and all about yourself—on the road to Troas.

*—The Cup and the Glory*, p. 48

## DEEPER WALK STUDY

For those who want to research additional related Scripture and topics, consider the following:

Second Corinthians contains at least two unique features. First, it reveals more of Paul's personal details (including his heart and some matters not found anywhere else) than do the other epistles. Second, this epistle contains more about spiritual warfare than do his other epistles, including Ephesians. Read 2 Corinthians and mark these (or write them on a sheet of paper), as well as events that would cause the apostle to be "perplexed but not despairing."

# Chapter Four

# The Gift

## SCRIPTURE REFERENCES

Key passages used in this chapter include: Philippians 1 (especially 1:29) and 2 Corinthians 8–9.

## READING ASSIGNMENTS

Read chapter four "The Gift" before attempting to answer any of the following questions.

## QUESTIONS FROM *THE CUP AND THE GLORY*

1. What is the importance of the verb *charidzomai* in describing this type of giving (pp. 51-52)?

   _____

   _____

   _____

   _____

2. Why do we have difficulty with a verse that indicates God can graciously give suffering (pp. 52-53)?

   _____

   _____

   _____

   _____

3. Why does Philippians 1:29 relate only to Christians? Explain (pp. 53-54).

   _____

   _____

   _____

   _____

4. How did God use the suffering of Paul and Silas in Acts 16 to His glory? Explain (pp. 55-56).

   _____

   _____

s seen in the previous statement from Jesus, the mindset of a loving father giving good gifts is not foreign to one's Heavenly Father. In fact, God is vastly superior to even the best earthly fathers because of His divine nature and the total absence of evil from Him. As evident throughout the totality of Scripture, God is by nature the God who gives. While the New Testament contains other words for giving, one particular word utilizes the same Greek word for "grace" and describes the type of giving often associated with God. The word *charidzomai* means "to give graciously" or "to bestow on one a favor or kindness."

—*The Cup and the Glory*, pp. 51-52

## QUESTIONS FROM THE WORD

1. Besides Philippians 1:29, what are some other verses used for the "grace gift?" What is the "grace gift" by God in the following verses: Galatians 3:18; Luke 7:21, 42; Rom. 8:3; 1 Cor. 2:12?

_____

_____

_____

_____

2. Is the power to believe actually given by God? Note: there is only one use of *charidzomai* ("grace given") in Philippians 1:29, but it is connected to two things given by God: (1) "not only to believe in Him" and (2) "but also to suffer for His sake."

_____

_____

_____

_____

3. How could suffering possibly be included with this grace gift to believe?

_____

_____

_____

_____

4. How could God permit the things that happened to a beloved servant like the Apostle Paul in 2 Corinthians 11:23-27? Was Paul not exercising sufficient faith to claim what was his under what some people call "The Prosperity Gospel" (pp. 54-55)?

_____

_____

_____

_____

5. What three Macedonian churches are found in Acts 16–17? Give the spiritual and physical characteristics of them from 2 Corinthians 8:1-9 (pp. 56-59).

_____

_____

_____

_____

cripture records another gift graciously given by God, but it is a gift no one requests. No one becomes envious when God bestows it on others, and no one anxiously awaits its arrival. Paul wrote to the Philippians of such a gift in one of the most intriguing statements in all Scripture: "For to you it has been granted/given [*charidzomai*] for Christ's sake, not only to believe in Him, but also to suffer for His sake" (Phil. 1:29). Paul utilized the same word for God giving suffering as he did for God giving His own Son to die (Rom. 8:32), as well as for the blessings associated with the Holy Spirit (1 Cor. 2:12). We gladly receive and welcome the first two given by God. On the other hand, not only do we not ask, we do not want "to be graciously given" suffering by God. Some "gift." When God gives us suffering, we would gladly return it and exchange it for something we really want, if we could ever get the heavenly store to open.

*—The Cup and the Glory*, p. 52

## THE HEART OF THE MATTER

By way of review, make sure that you are able to answer biblically the following questions. If you are not, go back and study again the appropriate sections.

1. Were the Philippians really "grace given" both the capacity to believe and to suffer? What are the implications of this?

_____

_____

_____

_____

2. What are two or three other verses which show the nature of *charidzomai* giving?

_____

_____

_____

_____

3. How were the Philippian Christians "grace gifted" by God? What does this teach in regard to the initial point of salvation as well as to the believer's walk? Explain.

_____

_____

_____

_____

## PERSONAL APPLICATION SECTION

1. When is suffering a gift from God? When is it not? Explain.

_____

_____

_____

_____

2. When would you tell someone else that suffering can be a gift from God? When would you not? When would you wait? Explain.

_____

_____

_____

_____

3. Were the Macedonian churches (2 Cor. 8:1-9) blessed or cursed by God? Explain. Would you be content if you evaluate your life by the same criteria? Explain.

_____

_____

_____

_____

4. Write your own personal application question from this chapter and give the answer.

_____

_____

he Macedonian churches had already formulated their viewpoint on giving to and receiving from God, which is why they gave so freely, even in the midst of intense suffering. Paul disclosed the secret of such a mindset in 2 Corinthians 8:5: "but they first gave themselves to the Lord." Again, the irony of true Christian giving shows itself. God does not want or need our money; He wants us. If He has us—our hearts, our passion, our drive—then money is no problem. Neither is time or commitment or sacrifice or inconvenience or suffering or walking by faith contrary to the world's methodology. When one first gives oneself to the Lord, the allurements of the world become less and less attractive and increasingly shallower. Not only this, but when an individual or a church gives themselves to the Lord, it is not so much characterized by ethereal sighings before God, but rather it becomes evident in their relationship with others around them. Sacrificial giving to others becomes as natural a correspondence as exhaling is to inhaling. In its simplest terms, when the Macedonian churches "first gave themselves to the Lord," it meant all which the world—even those in the Christian world—values and lecherously clings to was replaced by an all-encompassing desire to know Christ in a deeper and ever-increasing fashion. God blessed and honored such a desire to know Him on a level oblivious to most believers, and the results continue throughout eternity.

*—The Cup and the Glory*, p. 59

## DEEPER WALK STUDY

For those who want to research additional related Scripture and topics, consider the following:

First, in Acts 9:15-16, after Paul's conversion, the Lord instructs a hesitant Ananias, "Go, for he [Saul who would become Paul] is a chosen instrument of Mine, to bear My name before the Gentiles and kings and the sons of Israel, for I will show him how much he must suffer for My name's sake." Jesus already knows what Paul will suffer, when, and to what degree (which is another great sovereignty of God passage). Read Acts 9–28 and note the multiple examples where this proves true.

Second, what does God teach about true Christian giving in 2 Corinthians 8-9? Note especially the closing verse in reference to God's gift (2 Cor. 9:15).

Third, carefully read and write observations on Acts 16 and 2 Corinthians 8-9. Now read the Book of Philippians with this background and understanding.

# Chapter Five

# The Fellowship

## SCRIPTURE REFERENCES

Key passages used in this chapter include: John 20:17; Acts 2:42; Philippians 3 (especially 3:8-10); Mark 14:33-36.

## READING ASSIGNMENTS

Read chapter five "The Fellowship" before attempting to answer any of the following questions.

## QUESTIONS FROM *THE CUP AND THE GLORY*

1. What was biblically wrong with what the secular psychologist taught at the funeral (pp. 63-64)? Explain.

   _____

   _____

   _____

   _____

2. What were the three points Greg Harris used for the funeral that he performed (pp. 64-66)? What are the differences in the two funerals described in the chapter? Explain.

   _____

   _____

   _____

   _____

3. How did Paul "count" in Philippians 3:7-10? Give examples of how this was reflected in Paul's life (pp. 70-72).

   _____

   _____

   _____

   _____

4. What is the difference between suffering and "the fellowship of His sufferings" (pp. 70-73)? Explain.

_____

_____

_____

_____

5. Why do all Christians not suffer to the same degree (pp. 73-74)?

_____

_____

_____

_____

6. So what does "the fellowship of His sufferings" mean (p. 74)?

_____

_____

_____

_____

7. Describe what occurred in Gethsemane according to Mark's Gospel (pp. 76-77).

_____

_____

_____

_____

When Jesus and the disciples encountered a man born blind, the disciples had a logical question: Who sinned, the man or the man's parents? They assumed such misery must be directly related to the sins of someone, and they want to know who was to blame. The answer Jesus gave is at once both startling and comforting. In John 9:3 Jesus answered, "It was neither that this man sinned, nor his parents; but it was in order that the works of God might be displayed in him." We, too, must trust that answer. When someone dear to us dies—especially a child—we can scan the long list of our sins and shortcomings we have committed and conclude it must be God's hand of retribution against one of our more heinous acts. What grace God gives us as He calls us to look to Him instead of the unfathomable mysteries of sorrow and grief. What comfort in knowing we are not the cause of the death. God knows our beginning and our end from before the foundation of the world. He numbers our days by His sovereign counsel. While we should never take sin lightly or assume consequences do not follow our actions, we must look to a greater hope. Our focus should be on the promise of God that "neither this man sinned, nor his parents"—and look instead for God to display His works.

*—The Cup and the Glory, p. 65*

## QUESTIONS FROM THE WORD

1. What does the word "fellowship" mean? Why is the word absent from the Gospels? What is the significance of John 20:17 (pp. 66-67)?

_____

_____

_____

_____

2. Acts 2:42 is the first New Testament use of the word "fellowship." Why here? Why now? What has taken place in Acts 1:1–2:41?

_____

_____

_____

_____

3. List Paul's other uses for the word "fellowship" (pp. 67-68). What does each phrase mean?

_____

_____

_____

_____

4. How does Philippians 3:1-9 establish the basis for what Paul will write in 3:10 (pp. 70-71)? Explain.

_____

_____

_____

_____

5. What are the two aspects of knowing Jesus that Paul used in Philippians 3:10? Can these two be separated? Why or why not (pp. 71-72)?

_____

_____

_____

_____

6. Name the three uses of "Abba" in Scripture? Why only here? What does each verse teach (pp. 75-76)?

_____

_____

_____

_____

he Greek word *koinonia*, generally translated "fellowship," also means "participation, association, communion, sharers in." The word did not originate in the Christian world. Secular writings of the day used *koinonia* with roughly the same definition. However, with the birth of the Church, and primarily through the Holy Spirit, the word portrayed a unique and warm fellowship of unity in Christ. Strangely enough *koinonia* is completely absent from the Gospel accounts. Perhaps this is so the focus can be properly on the unique person and work of Jesus. John 1:14 records, "and the Word became flesh and dwelt [or "tabernacled"] among us." God incarnate in the flesh living among His creation was magnificent in itself, but still a void existed until Jesus completed our redemption. Full fellowship with God was only in the process of being opened when Jesus lived on the earth.

*—The Cup and the Glory*, pp. 65-66

## THE HEART OF THE MATTER

By way of review, make sure that you are able to answer biblically the following questions. If you are not, go back and study again the appropriate sections.

1. By way of review, what does the word "fellowship" mean? Why was the word "fellowship" not used in the Gospels except after the cross, the resurrection, the ascension and the pouring out of the Holy Spirit? What changed (pp. 66-68)?

_____

_____

_____

_____

2. Why would Paul use this word in Philippians 3:10? What do verses 7-10 teach (pp. 70-74)?

_____

_____

_____

_____

3. What is the significance of Jesus' use of "Abba" in Mark 14:33-36? From the text used, describe as best you can what Gethsemane was for Jesus (pp. 74-77).

_____

_____

_____

_____

*I*n Paul's estimation, fellowship began with God but carried over to personal relations within the Church. The same holds true today. Fellowship begins with God—not with others. Those who skip over the Cornerstone to enjoy "religious fellowship" with each other based on their own merits simply have a form of godliness, but they deny the power therein."

*—The Cup and the Glory, p. 68*

## PERSONAL APPLICATION SECTION

1. From what we have learned in this chapter, how does this affect your understanding of God and of your walk? Explain.

_____

_____

_____

_____

2. This chapter has deeply affected many people. Did it affect you, and if so, how and why were you affected? Explain.

_____

_____

_____

_____

3. What have you learned from this chapter that you want to tell someone else? Whom would you tell? Why?

_____

_____

_____

_____

4.  Write your own personal application question from this chapter (in other words, "what have I learned") that was not asked elsewhere and give the answer to your question.

_____

_____

_____

_____

*I* f you asked most Christians today what it would take for them to know Jesus better, the answers most likely would range from Bible study, time alone with God, prayer, a good church, good fellowship, seminars or Christian magazines. Most of these have varying validity, but in Paul's estimation, they lacked a key component. In Philippians 3:10 Paul wrote that I may "know Him." He used the Greek word that generally means, "to know by experience," rather than "to know intellectually." Herein is a foundational difference between Paul and many others. Some limit their knowledge of Jesus only to information. Scribble it in a notebook, take good notes, treat the Bible as an academic textbook—walk away and leave it when you want. For Paul, the Person of Jesus stayed in the forefront. He never denied the need for deep study—he enjoyed it—but he never divorced the doctrine from the Author. Living words from the living God nourished Paul throughout his Christian walk.

*—The Cup and the Glory, p. 71*

## DEEPER WALK STUDY

For those who want to research additional related Scripture and topics, consider the following:

Knowing what Philippians 3:10 teaches, read again Acts 16, 2 Corinthians 8–9, and Philippians 1–3. The chapters should "come alive" or "flesh out" when we note the bigger picture and the continuity of the Word.

# Chapter Six

# The Footprints

## SCRIPTURE REFERENCES

Key passages used in this chapter include: 1 Peter 1–2; John 13 (especially 1 Peter 2:21-25; John 13:31-38).

## READING ASSIGNMENTS

Read chapter six "The Footprints" before attempting to answer any of the following questions.

## QUESTIONS FROM *THE CUP AND THE GLORY*

1. How did God change Peter from the time of the Gospels until the time that he wrote 1 Peter? How has he grown (pp. 79-81)? Explain.

   _____

   _____

   _____

   _____

2. What was the trick question that Greg Harris often asked his classes, and why was it a trick question (pp. 81-82)?

   _____

   _____

   _____

   _____

3. What can we learn about God's work in Christians' lives from the word *hypogrammon* in 1 Peter 2:21, usually translated "example?" (Remember that the Greek word means "to write under.")

   _____

   _____

   _____

   _____

4. Contrast Peter's self-evaluation versus Jesus' divine evaluation of him. What can we learn from this (pp. 88-90)?

_____

_____

_____

_____

5. Where do the footprints of Jesus lead? Why there (p. 92)?

_____

_____

_____

_____

6. What is the importance of the statement, "you do not 'follow upon' the footprints by standing still" (pp. 92-93)? Explain.

_____

_____

_____

_____

ne difference in Peter at this point versus the Gospel years is he had become a shepherd, but not merely in response to Jesus' threefold injunction to him to feed His lambs. Peter was now a shepherd from the heart. The suffering Peter endured over the decades produced such a change. He no longer would be among those who argued over who was the greatest apostle. He no longer informed the Lord what will and will not be permissible, or boasted in his allegiance to Him. Peter demonstrated this in the care he exhibited for the flock scattered throughout Pontus, Galatia, Cappadocia, Asia and Bithynia. Interestingly, much of this region consisted of the area God forbade the Apostle Paul to enter in Acts 16. God had not rejected those people; He sent them Peter instead, all in accord with His precise orchestration.

—*The Cup and the Glory*, p. 81

## QUESTIONS FROM THE WORD

1. How does Peter begin his first epistle (1:1-12)? Why did he use the order that he did? Explain (pp. 82-83).

_____

_____

_____

_____

2. By means of observation of the text, list 10-15 things from 1 Peter 2:21-25 which Jesus did for His redeemed or else are true about Him.

_____

_____

_____

_____

3. What did Peter offer Jesus in John 13:31-38? Why did Jesus refuse Peter's offer? How does Jesus mildly rebuke Peter by what He said? Explain (pp. 88-90).

_____

_____

_____

_____

4. How does the Greek word *dynamai* show what Jesus was saying to His disciples? What did He mean by this (pp. 86-87)?

_____

_____

_____

_____

5. With some of the richness of the word studies given in this chapter, summarize the expanded thought of 1 Peter 2:21-25 (pp. 91-92).

_____

_____

_____

_____

*W*e need to consider what Jesus told them, especially since it would contradict Peter's personality to let what Jesus said go without further interrogation. Jesus informed the disciples they were unable, *dynamai* in the Greek, meaning they did not have the power or capability to go where He was going. As before, the word is where we get our modern word *dynamite*. It was not from a lack of permission the disciples could not accompany Jesus—it was from a lack of personal qualification. To go where Jesus would go was uniquely His. No doubt, to have had company would have lessened His anguish. However, as is true in Revelation 5, in all God's creation no one would be found worthy to walk the road He must walk, to drink the cup He must drink.

—*The Cup and the Glory*, p. 87

## THE HEART OF THE MATTER

By way of review, make sure that you are able to answer biblically the following questions. If you are not, go back and study again the appropriate sections.

1. How does Peter put the focus on the eternal in 1 Peter 1:1-12? Why does he do this (pp. 82-84)?

   _____

   _____

   _____

   _____

2. What are the major points of 1 Peter 2:21-25?

   _____

   _____

   _____

   _____

3. What is the significance of the word *hyper* used in both John 13:31-38 and 1 Peter 2:21-25? How does the perfect substitutionary work of Jesus show forth? Explain (pp. 88-91).

   _____

   _____

   _____

   _____

4. By way of review, why were the disciples not able (*dynamai*) to go where only Jesus could go (pp. 86-88)?

   _____

   _____

   _____

   _____

*W*hen you contemplate His suffering for us—or rather in place of us—it makes our suffering more bearable. Instead of concluding, "He does not know what I am going through," you have the solid assurance He does know and, in fact, knows better than we do in our limited capabilities can. Understanding the suffering of Jesus in even a little more depth changes our perspective, making us even worshipful in the midst of our own suffering. To put it as Paul did, instead of Jesus knowing about our suffering, we attain a certain amount of the fellowship of His suffering—and we are transformed from the inside out, as God wields this tool as a means of making us more Christ-like.

*—The Cup and the Glory, p. 91*

## PERSONAL APPLICATION SECTION

1. How did these rich spiritual truths found in John 13:31-38 and 1 Peter 2:21-25 impact your life? Explain.

_____

_____

_____

_____

2. Many Christians can identify with Peter. Is that true for you as well? Why? In what ways? Explain.

_____

_____

_____

_____

3. What can we learn about God from the use of *hypogrammon* ("example") in 1 Peter 2:21? What does He call us to do in regard to this? Does knowing about this help your walk, and if so, how? Explain.

_____

_____

_____

_____

4. Write your own personal application question from this chapter (in other words, "what have I learned") that was not asked elsewhere and give the answer to your question.

_____

_____

_____

_____

*I*n the previous context, Peter instructed slaves to submit to masters, even the unreasonable ones. He did not write this for the benefit of harmonious societal workings, nor for the benefit of the master. If ever a "why should I?" would emerge, it would be for a Christian slave to submit willingly to an unreasonable master, with many masters no doubt being unbelievers. How about you? Would you submit, willingly and from the heart? Probably not, especially not of your own initiative. Such exercised humility requires a higher calling. Peter always pointed to Jesus: He did this for you; you follow His example. No complaint registers long whenever Jesus is in view. "It's not fair. It's not right. I deserve better"—anyone want to argue their case above the one Jesus had? We will not be prone to either if we continually look to Jesus instead of our circumstances.

*—The Cup and the Glory, p. 84*

## DEEPER WALK STUDY

For those who want to research additional related Scripture and topics, consider the following:

Read all of 1 Peter in one sitting. Make special note of: (1) the order used in 1:1-12, (2) the rather brief doctrinal section before the application begins in 1:13 and following, and (3) the number of times Peter calls Christians to do something that is hard or odious (for example, "servants be submissive to masters" [2:18]), and then uses Jesus as the ultimate example of willful, submissive obedience (2:21-25). This occurs throughout the epistle.

## Chapter Seven

# The Surprise

### SCRIPTURE REFERENCES

Key passages used in this chapter include: 1 Peter 1-4; Job 1–2; especially 1 Peter 4:12-19.

### READING ASSIGNMENTS

Read chapter seven "The Surprise" before attempting to answer any of the following questions.

### QUESTIONS FROM *THE CUP AND THE GLORY*

1. Remember the background for the original recipients of 1 Peter. Why would it be difficult to harmonize 1 Peter 1:5 ("protected by the power of God") with 1 Peter 4:10 ("the fiery ordeal")? Explain (pp. 95-97).

   _____

   _____

   _____

   _____

2. What lessons can we understand about Jesus living all of His life without failing in any of the trials and temptation He endured? What would have happened if He had failed even once? Explain (pp. 101-102).

   _____

   _____

   _____

   _____

3. What was Jesus' prayer for Peter in Luke 22:32? Did it come true? How do you know (pp. 104)?

   _____

   _____

   _____

   _____

4. How did Peter show that he did not fully believe what Jesus said that would take place (pp. 104-105)? Explain.

_____

_____

_____

_____

5. How did the sifting affect Peter? Explain (pp. 105-106).

_____

_____

_____

_____

6. How could God allow His own Son to be tempted by Satan (pp. 106-107)?

_____

_____

_____

_____

7. How does 1 Peter 4:19 summarize what the present perspective of Christians should be? Explain (pp. 108-109).

_____

_____

_____

_____

*I*f God currently protected them, why were they suffering so intensely? Maybe God's protection was not what they thought it was, or maybe it had some holes in it. Yet this still did not match what they understood to be true about God's might and power, especially what they knew about His active love for them. They had good reason to be surprised, and Peter did not rebuke them for it.

What Peter did was take them deeper into the mind of God so they could consider suffering from God's perspective. While surprised at the degree of suffering they presently faced, they would be equally surprised at Peter's counsel to them.

—*The Cup and the Glory*, p. 96

## QUESTIONS FROM THE WORD

1. Read Job 1–2 and write ten biblical truths which we can learn from these two chapters.

   _____

   _____

   _____

   _____

2. The *peirasmos* tempting is usually one with an evil intent, looking for one to fail. Trace through Scripture the places where this word occurs (pp. 99-102).

   _____

   _____

   _____

   _____

3. Based on the question above, what verses from the ones disclosed in this chapter surprised you that it was this type of temptation? Why?

   _____

   _____

   _____

   _____

4. Review the parallel accounts in Luke 22:31 and John 13:31-38. What can we learn from Peter's thoughts and reasoning? Did he fully grasp what was about to happen? Explain (pp.102-103).

   _____

   _____

   _____

   _____

5. How does what is recorded in the Gospel accounts affect the way in which Peter wrote his epistle? Show some of their similarities (pp. 107-108).

   _____

   _____

   _____

   _____

e will never have the complete answers to such unanswerable questions during our lifetime. God does not necessarily promise us full disclosure, but then again, neither did He leave us in complete spiritual ignorance. For instance, observing the life of Job gives us a glimpse into one of the reasons faithful followers of God suffer. A spiritual warfare rages that is invisible to human cognizance, with Satan being the antagonist against God and His people, which includes us. We are a little more enlightened than Job, but not much. Since we also cannot see all the factors involved, we often are not certain about the origin or purpose of our suffering, especially when we are in the midst of it. No spiritual barometer exists which indicates this suffering is due to satanic influence, but this one is not. As was true for Job, circumstances limit us to only observing the symptoms of suffering and making our own limited deductions, which more likely will not be any more accurate that were those of Job. Graciously, God has chosen to reveal more information in Scripture about the surprise of suffering He permits on His own.

*—The Cup and the Glory*, p. 98

## THE HEART OF THE MATTER

By way of review, make sure that you are able to answer biblically the following questions. If you are not, go back and study again the appropriate sections.

1. By way of review, what is the type of temptation generally used for evil intent? Where are some verses in which this occurs (pp. 99-102)?

   _____

   _____

   _____

   _____

2. What occurred in Luke 22 that forever changed Simon Peter (pp. 102-106)?

   _____

   _____

   _____

   _____

3. How does what Peter learn show years later in his epistle? Explain (pp. 107-109).

   _____

   _____

   _____

   _____

ne mistake, one sinful response, one misuse of His power, one following through on a lust-ful thought, one selfish act, one wrong thing said—any inappropriate response to a *peirasmos* testing, and our Lamb would become blemished, our Shepherd soiled, our Savior disqualified. Gethsemane and Calvary are magnificent demonstrations of the love and majesty of Jesus so beyond our human understanding that we could more easily perceive the full scope of God's cre-ation than we could the depths of His love displayed there. But for Jesus to live every day of His life in sinless perfection; to receive the totality of satanic assault and temptation, yet never stum-ble or trip; to press on in obedience to God's leading, even when the leading resulted in severe suffering, and sufferings eventually lead to death—we are speechless in awe, or at least should be. When the *peirasmos* onslaughts pulverize us and we suffer, we realize to a much clearer degree our own limitations, weaknesses and the need for God's engulfing grace. We have a better under-standing of the strength of Jesus, realizing how quickly we fall and stumble with only a billionth of what He endured. If you follow God's design, suffering will make you more appreciative and worshipful of the Savior and intimately closer to Him. We realize only limited suffering in our lives often causes us to respond poorly, recognizing our total ineptitude to comprehend the extent of His suffering in our behalf, and yet remain without sin. Not only could we not endure His testing, we cannot even begin to perceive of their magnitude.

*—The Cup and the Glory, p. 102*

## PERSONAL APPLICATION SECTION

1. Is "the surprise" verse of 1 Peter 4:12 surprising to you? Why or why not?

_____

_____

_____

_____

2. What lessons can we learn from the fact that God permitted Satan to attack Job in Job 1–2? Is this surprising to you? Why or why not?

_____

_____

_____

_____

3. How is your understanding of trials and suffering different, knowing that there are different words used to indicate the origin of or the reason for the trial? Explain.

_____

_____

_____

_____

4. What have you learned from this chapter that you want to tell someone else? Whom would you tell? Why?

_____

_____

_____

_____

5. Write your own personal application question from this chapter (in other words, "what have I learned") that was not asked elsewhere and give the answer to your question.

_____

_____

_____

_____

o only months before his own martyrdom, Peter's counsel to his fellow-sufferers was, "Do not be surprised at the fiery ordeal that comes upon you for your testing." The victory is won, but the battles continue. We acknowledge this concept in theory, but it still surprises us when suffering surrounds us—but it really should not. The servant is not above his Master. We are sharers of His suffering, and will be shares of His glory. Not only should we actively endure by trusting God, but also if we get our perspective in line with God's the result of such suffering can be a matter of great joy for us. The joy goes beyond simply having the suffering end. Even beyond these other considerations is one underlying truth we need to explore: God uses *peirasmos* trials for the express purpose so He may bless us.

—*The Cup and the Glory*, p. 109

## DEEPER WALK STUDY

For those who want to research additional related Scripture and topics, consider the following:

Trace Peter from Luke 22 through Acts 4. Specifically mark his failures, Jesus' rebuilding of him, and how he is an entirely different man only weeks later. Although not suitable for every situation, what can one learn from Peter's failure and restoration? Explain.

For those who have the biblical tools, consider tracing the words which Jesus said in the Gospels and list how many are used by Peter later in his first and second epistles.

# Chapter Eight

# The Blessing

## SCRIPTURE REFERENCES

Key passages used in this chapter include: Genesis 32; James 1 (especially 2-3); 1 Peter 1 (especially 6-7).

## READING ASSIGNMENTS

Read chapter eight "The Blessing" before attempting to answer any of the following questions.

## QUESTIONS FROM *THE CUP AND THE GLORY*

1. What can we learn from God's wrestling with Jacob in Genesis 32? Give some examples (pp. 111-13).

_____

_____

_____

_____

2. Why are the blessings in the Beatitudes (Matt. 5:1-12) contrary to our definition of blessing (pp. 115-16)?

_____

_____

_____

_____

3. Explain what we learn about the process that God often employs to bless us (pp. 115-17).

_____

_____

_____

_____

4. Describe the background of James. What are some of his characteristics (pp. 118-20)?

_____

_____

_____

_____

5. How is what James wrote similar to 1 Peter? How does it differ and why? Explain (pp. 120-21).

_____

_____

_____

_____

6. Expand the meaning of "steadfast endurance." What did James write concerning this (pp. 121-22)?

_____

_____

_____

_____

> Rarely in Scripture, if at all, does one receive great blessings of God or is one used tremendously by Him without wrestling with God through pain, disappointment, despondency, loneliness or suffering. Although quite painful during the process, all such prolonged testing occurs for the express purpose of God refining and blessing us.
>
> —*The Cup and the Glory*, p. 113

## QUESTIONS FROM THE WORD

1. List some Old Testament examples of godly individuals who had to learn patient endurance and obedience in order for God to bless them greatly.

_____

_____

_____

_____

2. Define the Greek word *makarios* ("blessed"). List some of the Scripture references for this word and what the verses teach (pp. 114-15).

_____

_____

_____

_____

3. What can we learn about the words used in James 1:2-3 and 1 Peter 1:6-7 about the different nature of trials? Explain (p. 117).

_____

_____

_____

_____

4. From these chapters, expand the fuller meaning of James 1:2-3 and 1 Peter 1:6-7. Paraphrase in your own words what these verses mean.

_____

_____

_____

_____

God allows tests in our lives for us to pass, not looking for us to fail. For instance, we claim we have faith in God. God allows or brings tests into our lives so that we may give evidence of the genuineness of our faith. Such tests, however, move us far beyond our comfort zone. The "proof of your faith" will stretch you in ways you never have been, and in ways you never knew you could.

—*The Cup and the Glory*, p. 117

## THE HEART OF THE MATTER

By way of review, make sure that you are able to answer biblically the following questions. If you are not, go back and study again the appropriate sections.

1. How does God's definition of blessing differ from ours? Explain some of the uses of the word "blessed," such as those found in the Beatitudes of Matthew 5:1-12.

_____

_____

_____

_____

2. What is the difference between the two words used for "trial" or "testing" used in this chapter of the book and in the previous chapter?

_____

_____

_____

_____

3. By way of review, explain how Peter and James use both words in 1 Peter 1:6-7 and James 1:2-3 and why knowing this is so important.

_____

_____

_____

_____

4. What is the biblical concept of "steadfast endurance?" Show some Scripture examples in which this word is used.

_____

_____

_____

_____

One reason this is so incompatible with our way of thinking is our definition of blessing often differs considerably from God's definition of blessing. While our perception of blessing may have a spiritual element to it, most of us view blessings from God largely in the earthly or physical realm: health, safety, possessions, etc.

Again, these are valid to a degree, and we should look to God as our Provider and Giver. But God has a more elevated perception of blessing. God sees the total scope of future history, looking at eternal consequences, whereas we are mostly limited, both by choice and by design, to the temporal.

—*The Cup and the Glory*, p. 115

## PERSONAL APPLICATION SECTION

1. How did your understanding of blessing (*makarios*) change with the 1 Peter verses which used this word? How about Jesus' use of it in the Beatitudes of Matthew 5? Would you consider your self blessed? Explain.

_____

_____

_____

_____

2. How is your understanding of trials and suffering different, knowing that there are different words used to indicate the origin of or the reason for the trial? (This is similar to what is asked in chapter seven, but now you have a broader biblical framework). Explain.

_____

_____

_____

_____

3. Why are the truths in this chapter primarily for self-examination before you attempt to evaluate someone else's situation? Explain (pp. 122-23).

_____

_____

_____

_____

4. From this chapter, what would you share with someone else?

_____

_____

_____

_____

5. Write your own personal application question from this chapter (in other words, "what have I learned") that was not asked elsewhere and give the answer to your question.

_____

_____

_____

_____

God sees the complete picture and can therefore see blessings He has ahead of us, as well as the route He must take us to bring us there, even when we see only darkness. Yet, this very process adds to our confusion because most of our sufferings involve the loss of something or someone precious to us. Since our perception of blessing often relates largely to physical matters, the temporary removal of such physical blessings intensifies our suffering. It causes us to consider ourselves anything but blessed of God. We can perceive God's blessing in the lives of others, but sometimes it is hard to see it in our own lives, especially in the midst of deep suffering.

—*The Cup and the Glory*, p. 116

## DEEPER WALK STUDY

For those who want to research additional related Scripture and topics, consider the following:

First, read all of James and 1 Peter and list their similarities and contrasts. Make special note of the backgrounds of the different authors that we have seen in different chapters of the book.

Second, Paul frequently uses "steadfast endurance" (*hypomenes*). If you have a concordance, look up "endurance" or "endure" and write the way Paul uses this in his epistles. You may want to summarize your findings about what Paul teaches regarding this necessary Christian virtue.

# Chapter Nine

# The Agreement

## SCRIPTURE REFERENCES

Key passages used in this chapter include: 1 Peter 5:1-10.

## READING ASSIGNMENTS

Read chapter nine "The Agreement" before attempting to answer any of the following questions.

## QUESTIONS FROM *THE CUP AND THE GLORY*

1. Explain why it is vital to read 1 Peter 5:6-9 before "claiming the promise" of 5:10 (p. 131).

_____

_____

_____

_____

2. What is true biblical humility? Why is this often so hard to live out in our life? Explain (p. 132).

_____

_____

_____

_____

3. Explain the similarities and differences between what James and Peter wrote regarding humbling oneself (pp. 132-33).

_____

_____

_____

_____

4. What did Peter write about Satan (5:8-9)? Explain why it is included in this portion (pp. 135-36).

_____

_____

_____

_____

5.  Show examples of how Peter used his own failure to teach and to encourage his readers (pp. 136-37).

_____

_____

_____

_____

owever, 1 Peter 5:6-9 delineates the believer's role and responsibility. They give the requirements for the believer before addressing God's promises. We are prone to claim the promises of a verse like First Peter 5:10, and then wonder why God does not respond as we expect. We examine Him, but are less inclined to scrutinize our own lives, to strengthen our own weakness and adjust where needed, to continue in faith. Simply put, God's promises of rebuilding in 5:10 occur once the believer lives out the elements of 5:6-9. Our examination begins with ourselves—not with God—but remember, it leads to a promise.

—*The Cup and the Glory*, p. 131

## QUESTIONS FROM THE WORD

1.  What does "casting all your anxiety on Him" mean in 1 Peter 5:7? What does Peter mean by the way he wrote it? Explain (pp. 134-35).

_____

_____

_____

_____

2.  Explain what "being sober" and " be on the alert" entail (pp. 135-36).

_____

_____

_____

_____

3.  List the "spiritual checklist" before we come to 1 Peter 5:10. Give references for each (pp. 131-137).

_____

_____

_____

_____

4. Paraphrase the four verbs relating to rebuilding in 5:10. What have you learned (pp. 140-42)?

_____

_____

_____

_____

5. Based on our studies and the context, explain in detail what 1 Peter 5:10 teaches (pp. 137-42).

_____

_____

_____

_____

*W*hile the promises of 1 Peter 5:10 hold true for those who steadfastly endure suffering, we never box in or corner God. God is not a mathematical formula that works the same every time. He has different and unique plans for us, including when and how we will go home to be with Him. We should plan to have a long and fruitful life, but we are also to have our spiritual bags packed and be ready for either His arrival or our departure.

—*The Cup and the Glory*, p. 139

### THE HEART OF THE MATTER

By way of review, make sure that you are able to answer biblically the following questions. If you are not, go back and study again the appropriate sections.

1. Explain biblically why believers not only should read 1 Peter 5:10 but also should expect God to work.

_____

_____

_____

_____

2. Explain in detail how a believer should prepare (1 Peter 5:5-9) before expecting God to work.

_____

_____

_____

_____

3. Give an expanded paraphrase of what 1 Peter 5:10 teaches.

_____

_____

_____

_____

> *P*eter's rationale for such casting was "because He (God) cares for you." Sometimes accepting the fact God cares for you is particularly difficult to do. At times all our circumstances of suffering seem to indicate that God does not do anything, especially actively care for us—but He does. True humility believes and accepts by faith that God lovingly and consistently works, even when we cannot see or feel any evidence that He does. Stand firm.
>
> —*The Cup and the Glory*, p. 135

## PERSONAL APPLICATION SECTION

1. Why do you think the author titled this chapter "The Agreement?" Do you think it's appropriate? Why?

_____

_____

_____

_____

2. After examining the text, write any specific areas in your life that you need to put into action in order to be obedient to what God commanded in 1 Peter 5:6-9. You may want to review this list to remind yourself of the items listed, or you may review the ways you have changed and have noted God's faithfulness. Don't be surprised if your list changes as you add and delete matters over time.

_____

_____

_____

_____

3. Based on the previous question, what keeps us from fulfilling 1 Peter 5:6-9? Explain.

_____

_____

_____

_____

4. From this chapter, what would you like to share with someone else? Whom would you tell? Why?

_____

_____

_____

_____

5. Write your own personal application question from this chapter (in other words, "what have I learned") that was not asked elsewhere and give the answer to your question.

_____

_____

_____

_____

> *I*f you are suffering, God has given you specific elements to expect. He Himself will perfect, confirm, strengthen and establish us. All are words of rebuilding and making strong that which is not. It points to His strength, not one's self-effort. He gives us more than hope—He gives us Himself. Peter's exhortation in 5:12 calls us to exhibit faith in action: "I have written to you briefly, exhorting and testifying that this is the true grace of God. Stand firm in it!" We should—and we must. God gives us the victory, but He chooses to rebuild and remake us in the process. Stand firm.
>
> —*The Cup and the Glory*, p. 142

## DEEPER WALK STUDY

For those who want to research additional related Scripture and topics, consider the following:

Trace the passages used in the Gospel that are in 1 Peter 5. Make sure you note the context for each verse used.

Read again all of 1 Peter and note all the different aspects of the study that we have seen thus far. It will be a continually growing delight as the book unfolds with a better understanding of it.

# Chapter Ten

# The Glory

## SCRIPTURE REFERENCES

Key passages used in this chapter include: Exodus 32–34; 1 Kings 18–19; Matthew 16–17.

## READING ASSIGNMENTS

Read chapter ten "The Glory" before attempting to answer any of the following questions.

## QUESTIONS FROM *THE CUP AND THE GLORY*

1. List some of the lessons we derive from Scripture about God's glory (pp. 146-48).

_____

_____

_____

_____

2. Upon initial consideration, why did God bring Moses and Elijah to the Transfiguration (pp. 148-49)?

_____

_____

_____

_____

3. Why was the victory of Elijah in 1 Kings 18 followed by spiritual failure in 1 Kings 19 (pp. 152-54)? Explain the significance.

_____

_____

_____

_____

4. What is the significance of Jesus and His disciples being in Caesarea Philippi when He asked, "Who do people say the Son of Man is" in Matthew 16:13? How is the setting suitable for what Jesus was about to teach His disciples (pp. 155-58)?

_____

_____

_____

_____

5.  Why is Matthew 16:27 the first time Jesus spoke of the glory of God in reference to Himself? What happened in Matthew 16 that led Him to say this at this time? Explain what occurs next (pp. 159-161).

_____

_____

_____

_____

6.  Explain why the Transfiguration is so important (p. 161).

_____

_____

_____

_____

7.  Further develop your understanding regarding why God had Moses and Elijah come to the Transfiguration (pp. 164-65). How has your understanding changed since you have read more? Explain.

_____

_____

_____

_____

*W*hat exactly is God's glory? We understand to a certain degree what comprises suffering, but glory is a different matter. The Bible frequently depicts glory as rightly belonging to God, as well as glory believers will receive in the future. Still, knowing God's glory exists is not the same as comprehending it. Like many topics in Scripture, God gives us only a partial revelation and limited information. He most likely restricts His revelation because it would not make sense to us until we are in His presence. Often the truths God reveals only lead to more questions, most of which cannot be fully answered until we go to be with the Lord. In response to the deeper questions of life, God gives us what He wants us to know and says in essence, "Trust Me" for the rest. We must—and we do.

—*The Cup and the Glory*, p. 146

## QUESTIONS FROM THE WORD

1. Read the accounts of Exodus 32-33 and describe what occurred in these chapters. Was Exodus 34 a fulfillment of Moses' request to have God show him His glory (pp. 149-151)? Explain the significance.

_____

_____

_____

_____

2. Who is "the angel of the LORD" in 1 Kings 19:7? Why is this so important (pp. 153-54)?

_____

_____

_____

_____

3. Describe the events which took place in 1 Kings 19:1-11 (pp. 154-55).

_____

_____

_____

_____

4. What is the significance of God's statement as expressed in Scripture through Peter in Matthew 16:13-17? How is this different from previous statements that Peter said, and why is this so important (pp. 156-58)? Explain.

_____

_____

_____

_____

5. How does Matthew 16 set the stage for the Transfiguration in Matthew 17:1-8? Explain.

_____

_____

_____

_____

6.  How did the Transfiguration affect Peter and what he wrote in his final epistle? Show examples (pp. 165-66).

_____

_____

_____

_____

*N* ow Jesus took the teaching deeper; now He associated the glory of God with Himself and with His reign—and He did so beginning at the Transfiguration. The Transfiguration served not only as a confirming sign to Peter's Holy Spirit-inspired declaration of Matthew 16:16, but also as a preview of the glory that would one day be manifested to the entire world. Jesus will return to earth "in His glory, and the glory of the Father and of the holy angels" (Luke 9:26; also Matt. 16:27; Mark 8:38). The three Gospel accounts each preview and connect the Transfiguration with Jesus' revelation concerning His glory.

*—The Cup and the Glory, p. 161*

## THE HEART OF THE MATTER

Be able to answer the following questions biblically. If you unable to review the appropriate sections.

1.  Be able to describe the life of Moses (Exodus 32–34). It enables us to understand God's glory.

_____

_____

_____

_____

2.  Describe the events in the life of Elijah as seen in 1 Kings 18–19.

_____

_____

_____

_____

3.  Know the importance of Caesarea Philippi as the setting for the Jesus' teaching in Matthew 16.

_____

_____

_____

_____

4. Make sure that you can explain the importance of the events which took place in Matthew 16 which lead to the Transfiguration. Explain why this is so important.

_____

_____

_____

_____

oses and Elijah—plus every Old Testament saint from Adam onward—needed a Redeemer. Without the appropriate propitiation ["covering of sin"], God must hold them accountable for the totality of their own sins—and no one of the human race would ever have fellowship with God throughout eternity. Without the atonement there would be no salvation; hell would await everyone born, life being only a daily trek closer to damnation. Moses and Elijah would not instruct Jesus concerning His sacrificial death; if anything they would thank Him in advance.

—*The Cup and the Glory*, p. 164

### PERSONAL APPLICATION SECTION

1. Does your life resemble in any way Moses' desires in Exodus 32–34? If so, how? Explain.

_____

_____

_____

_____

2. What can we learn from God's physical and spiritual provisions for Elijah? Have there been such times for you? If so, bring them to mind, write them, and thank God for them. (We need to be reminded from time to time of His ongoing faithfulness to us).

_____

_____

_____

_____

3. In the same chapter where Jesus first announced His own death (Matt. 16:21), He also announced three requirements necessary for anyone to follow Him (Matt. 16:24-25). What are these three requirements? Are you currently doing them? How do you know? Explain.

_____

_____

_____

_____

4. How did the glory of God change Peter, James, and John? How does it change you? Explain.

_____

_____

_____

_____

5. Write your own personal application question from this chapter (in other words, "what have I learned") that was not asked elsewhere and give the answer to your question.

_____

_____

_____

_____

uffering can produce a yearning for the Bright Morning Star. Suffering tends to make us look to others for help and support—Jesus desires a large part of such looking to be directed toward Him. As Peter admonished his readers, "Fix your hope completely on the grace to be brought to you at the revelation ["uncovering"] of Jesus." He remains faithful. Stand firm.

—*The Cup and the Glory*, p. 170

## DEEPER WALK STUDY

For those who want to research additional related Scripture and topics, consider the following:

First, trace the angel of the LORD throughout the Old Testament. Note the activities which He does that God alone can do.

Second, read all the Transfiguration accounts, the entire epistle of 1 Peter, and then 2 Peter. Note again how much the training by Jesus during the Gospels affected the life and works of Peter.

# End of Study

# Summary Questions

1. List four or five significant matters which you have learned. Explain how they have affected your life.

   _____

   _____

   _____

   _____

   _____

   _____

   _____

   _____

2. How is your understanding of God different? Explain and give three or four examples.

   _____

   _____

   _____

   _____

   _____

   _____

   _____

3. How is your understanding of yourself different? Explain and give examples.

   _____

   _____

   _____

   _____

   _____

   _____

_____

_____

4. With whom do you look forward to sharing what you have learned in this study? Why?

_____

_____

_____

_____

_____

_____

5. From what you have learned in your study, write what you are thankful to God for. It could be something He already has done in your life or something He has promised in His Word to do.

_____

_____

_____

_____

_____

_____

6. By the way, what do you pray for . . . when you pray?

_____

_____

_____

_____

_____

_____

_____

# Q & A

# Interview with Betsy Harris

Many times through personal encounters or by correspondence people have asked me various questions about my wife Betsy and how she did through all this. Below are Betsy's responses to questions generally asked.

**Q**    Betsy, obviously parts of your story are similar to Greg's because you shared common experiences. How are they similar, and how are they different?

**A**    We shared grief as parents of the twins. I don't know if you can know exactly what the other is going through or that our grief could be separated or compared. For instance, how do you gauge the difference in grief between that of a Mom and that of a Dad? I think God alone knows the depths of how each one responds to our sufferings.

With Greg's arthritis I could only stand on the sideline and watch it but not feel it. It was very hard to watch. So, in a way, this was a shared experience, but it was one that affected us differently.

Being in "The Wilderness," when Greg was put on the shelf ministry-wise was by far the hardest period of our marriage. It just seemed that God brought everything to a dead end, and that there never would be an end to what we were going through. It affected every part of our life. That was the time where there was the least hope for either of us. It had been a long, long time (from our way of thinking).

**Q**    Greg wrote about being in "The Wilderness." Did you think that true for you and, if so, how was it? In other words, was your wilderness the same as his? Did you ever give up hope?

**A**    The answer to these questions sort of ties in with the response to the previous question. It was hard for me to explain to others what was going on in our lives and even less why. We certainly didn't see the big picture of what God was doing. When Greg worked in Charlotte for a year with a small group of men, that was hard to explain to others (especially relatives) as well. God took us both on a vastly different path than what we expected.

After many years not doing so, I resumed teaching school when Greg went on disability. I had stayed at home with the birth of Lauren and then returned to school when Ben started going to kindergarten. I taught at their school, and they rode in with me. It was such a hard adjustment. Both Greg and I have the utmost sympathy and appreciation for single parent moms or dads.

When Greg came off disability, we lived in North Carolina and he began to teach in Washington

DC and was gone three nights a week. Then there was the year when he was away in Charlotte during the week. It was a whirlwind of one thing right after another. The lots of different balls we had to juggle can wear you out. I was so overwhelmed at times.

 What was your low point(s) along the way?

 When I look back on those years, it seems to be more of looking at a segment of our lives versus one particular item. I look back at this somewhat as you would a package. So there was not one particular low point that stands out among the many. In some cases, it was just the continued drudgery of persevering.

I do remember my first Sunday after Greg got out of the hospital, something about the music being played in church just made me loose it as I wept and wept. It was probably just a culmination of everything finally hitting me.

 Were there any high points along the way?

 I think the high point for me is how Greg got on faculty at Southeastern (Baptist Theological Seminary). It was so neat how he told us about it that night at supper. We lived less than a mile from that beautiful campus, and every time I rode by I prayed that God would place Greg there full time. Our daughter Lauren was actually the most persistent prayer about this in our family. She was age 5-7 at the time.

Greg told us as we all stood in the kitchen holding hands and praying before supper. He prayed items to be thankful for and then included in his prayer, "And dear Lord, thank you so much for finally opening the door and allowing me to teach at Southeastern."

 So what did you think and do when Greg prayed and thanked God?

 We all opened our eyes and smiled. Lauren breathed in with astonishment. I think we wanted to make sure that Greg was not teasing us—and he was not. He would teach in the fall.

As far as looking back on the high points, there were so many acts of kindnesses extended, especially during Greg's arthritis. Some anonymous somebody mowed our grass once. Greg's old tree cutting group donated money. I found out later that many unsolicited checks arrived virtually every week without fail to help with the medical bills.

 How was it being a wife of someone with arthritis? Were there scary moments in the hospital?

𝒜    Greg was so sick when he went to the hospital, and they were not sure at all what he had. They initially thought it was bacterial endocarditis (where bacteria becomes lodged in his heart and is pumped out to different places in the body), and that it could possibly be life-threatening. As it turned out, it was not this but rheumatoid arthritis. But they didn't know at the time and were trying to prepare me for the worse.

One of the hardest times was when one of the doctors told Greg he would probably never run again and possibly not walk normally again. Greg called me from his hospital bed right after the doctor left his room and was crying. It was so sad to hear this from him and somewhat fearful.

It was also hard to watch him be in that much consuming pain, both at the hospital and once he came home. There just wasn't anything I could do other than try to make him as comfortable as possible. It was also almost like having a child (at times) that you had to take care of. There are little things that you take for granted when both the husband and the wife are both healthy. Little things even like no help with bringing in the groceries.

𝒬    With the death of the twins, were there things that people said that were helpful? Were there things that were not? Could you share some of what you remember?

𝒜    We had a pastor and friend in Maryland, Jeff Watson, who told us, "Don't expect this to be something you get over quickly. There will be a part of your that will never get over it." His words helped me when I felt like I should be feeling better and didn't. I don't really remember how long it took to get over the initial phase of grief.

We try to give people an accurate description when we talk about it. The loss of the twins was a deep, deep grief, but our children Lauren and Ben were both such delights. Lauren was four and Ben was almost three at the time. There were so many times where we laughed and played with them in one room and would go and weep in another room and then come back and play again.

Also a friend and a professor whom Greg worked with, Chris Doerfler, who was also one of the editors of the book, wrote a card and said, "Doesn't it make heaven seem so much more real?" That simple question was a wonderfully comforting and an accurate description.

I don't remember particularly anything that offended me, but it really did stand out with what people said whether they were walking with the Lord or not.

We did, however, have a family gathering where a well-intended relative called me up to stand up in front of a group shortly after the twins died and said, "Greg and Betsy have lost twins girls. Betsy, could you stand up and say a few words?" Greg was somewhere else (I forget where he was that day). I said, "Sir, what would like me to say?" It was awful; just terrible. We very much encourage others not to do that to someone else.

𝒬    Now that you are years removed from the events described in *The Cup and the Glory*, what did you learn about God during this time?

*A*    What I held on to was that God was sovereign and that He was good, even when my emotions strongly told me otherwise. I also knew that somehow God was going to work things out for His own glory and our good, and with that of the twins.

When you go through such hard times, if your commitment is not there beforehand as an established point, it can make shambles of your marriage. In other words, as much as possible, your commitment should be worked out ahead of time, if you can. You don't wait until you are in the midst of your most severe trials and tests.

*Q*    What did you learn about yourself?

*A*    I guess the two things that stand out are one, as Greg often says, so much of what we sing at church we don't really mean or understand what is required about standing or surrendering to God. Second, we are by no means as strong as we think we are during the brighter times.

*Q*    As you look back, when you see others going through similar situations, what do you tell them?

*A*    Everything that happened to us, there are so many situations that are worse. We very much know people who have suffered a great deal more than we have.

There are so many more good resources available now and the means to distribute them than before. The first time I ever heard the word "Internet" was when the doctors first diagnosed the twins' medical problem and told us the girls would not live. There are some wonderfully helpful materials available, such as John MacArthur's three-part series on the death of a child that are so much more accessible.

Also, there is still such a sense of loss for miscarriage or stillborn babies that often people you are around don't understand. Someone said something well meaning to Greg, but was so off base when they told him, "At least you didn't have time to love them." You do grieve because you do love them. You also grieve for your future you thought you would have. It is a very hard and sad thing to do to undecorate a nursery that you had prepared to bring home your baby to.

I also tell them that this will be a part of your testimony both of what God does for you personally in bringing you through it as well as how you will minister to others in the same situation. If they walk with the Lord through whatever He allows in their life, there will by so many ways that God will eventually use it in the life of others.

I also try to encourage them to keep their walk close with God and keep their focus on eternity.

# The Writing of The Cup and the Glory

The proceeds from *The Cup and the Glory* go to the Roland Lee Memorial Scholarship Fund in Bible Exposition. For information or to make a contribution, contact:

Washington Bible College
6511 Princess Garden Parkway
Lanham, MD 20706-3599
(301) 552-1400 ext. #1255
www.bible.edu

Roland Lee was a man of God. That is the simplest and best description I can make of him. I first met Roland when he was in my classes at Washington Bible College. I don't remember which class or even when it was; I don't even remember meeting him. Somewhere along the way we became friends. Appropriately enough, and keeping consistent in my pattern, I don't remember when we became friends—we just did.

I do know when I first spent the most time with him. I was returning to teaching after my seven-month disability from arthritis in January of 1996. I rode from Wake Forest, NC to Washington, DC with "the storm of the century" snow clouds in my rearview mirror. You know it is going to be a bad storm when the snow clouds are bluish black. In some places the snow level was four feet or more. The storm was so massive that the US government shut down for a week. My January class at the college was also postponed for a week. So, with the exception of a few people, I was alone at the college. I could not wear shoes yet, which was a shame because I would have loved to have played and ventured out in the snow.

During this time Roland invited me to eat with him and his wife De at their apartment that was on the Washington Bible College property. We had many extended conversations that week as Roland repeatedly invited me back to visit and eat with them. I felt embarrassed about repeatedly doing so, but I just enjoyed the fellowship so much.

Roland had quite a story by that time. He had awaken one morning at age 16 with kidney failure. Roland had been a very good athlete, but his life changed forever from that day onward. To this day they have never found the cause. His mom had given him one of her kidneys; his body rejected it after only a week. He received another kidney while he was in his mid-twenties. Rather quickly that kidney also quit working. Roland had to go on dialysis, which turned out to be an excruciating treatment for him. He very well knew that he would not live an extended life, by man's standards.

So, surrounded by blankets of snow, Roland and I spent more time together that January week than in all of our previous times combined. I was in the midst of the wilderness, and Roland was in his own wilderness as well, and he had less than three years to live. Some of the most blessed and edifying exchanges I have ever had occurred during that time. Looking back on it, I wish I had recorded the conversations or had taken notes. Also looking back on it, I am quite sure I got the better end of the deal with the friendship.

As you will see, Roland was the first person with whom I ever discussed much of what I was learning that eventually became *The Cup and the Glory*. He was the first one who strongly and repeatedly encouraged me to write what I was learning (which I was writing), but he greatly exhorted me even more to do so. So, a lot of what I wrote, although I wrote with myself in mind, I could not help but think, "Roland is going to *love* this!"—and he did—because Roland was a lover of God's Word.

If God somehow allowed me a conversation with anyone in heaven, other than with some biblical characters, I would pick Roland as the one. We would pick up our conversations where they left off. I love my parents, and I look forward to seeing them again in heaven, but I would love to talk over with Roland much of what we talked over about heaven, life, God, etc. We both, no doubt, saw at best in our wilderness conversations only in a mirror dimly. Roland currently dwells in the presence of the Lord. I'll catch up with him one day, soon perhaps.

Roland Lee's earthly life ended on August 10, 1999. He was 35 years old. I never thought it right to say, "Roland died"—which is technically accurate—but it is not descriptive of the man. Roland touched more lives during his relatively brief earthly walk than most people I know. I don't know if you could separate the love and admiration that the faculty and staff had for him from that of the student body. Everybody just loved him. Everyone admired him so. His laugh was infectious; his desire for God and His Glory were even more so. To this day there remains a "Roland Lee slice of my heart" missing.

I pray that God will raise up with the scholarship, for lack of better terms, "another Roland Lee." I am praying for fruit from the books, and part of the fruit is a young Roland out there who possesses the same insatiable hunger and thirst for God. Please pray that God honors this request, and please recommend someone to the school if you think he or she has the "Roland Lee potential."

### Timeframe of Events:

| | |
|---|---|
| March 25, 1993 | Death of our Twins |
| June 5, 1995 | Admitted to the hospital with arthritis |
| June-Dec. 1995 | On disability for seven months; Roland Lee covered my classes |
| May 1996 | Resigned from Washington Bible College; began "the work" in Charlotte, NC with Mike and Brenda Sprott (Tues/Wed) through July 27, 1997 |

Oct. 18, 1996          Scheduled to speak in chapel at Washington Bible College

Oct-Dec. 1996          Wrote what would become *The Cup and the Glory*

August 1, 1997          Began full-time at Southeastern Baptist Theological Seminary

Somewhere toward the end of the first week of October 1996, the wilderness ended. Perhaps stated better, it was not so much that the wilderness ended; rather, God brought me through *and* out of the wilderness. I know precisely the moment it ended. I was sitting at our breakfast nook at our house in Wake Forest, NC. I knew it was over; it was that definitive. There may be different aspects in the future, but I knew beyond any doubt that this particular wilderness was over. By the way, I never called it "The Wilderness" during the time I was in it. I didn't know what "it" was.

When "The Wilderness" ended I worshiped and praised God in abject silence and wonder—and repentance. It was not so much that a particular timeframe ended but rather that I came out differently from it (as others have come and will come out). It was though my mind exploded with Scripture (I don't know how to describe it otherwise). After about three days of worshipful silence before God, I prayed, "Lord, if this is what it takes for You to accomplish Your will in my life, then please put me back in line." My circumstances had not changed; my perception of God and His worthiness and my utter unworthiness had changed for all eternity.

In much too long a story, I ended up working with Mike Sprott for a year after I resigned from Washington Bible College. I helped him and his family and some of his workers study the Bible. I stayed with Mike and his wife Brenda on Tuesday nights in Charlotte, NC, about a three-hour drive from where I lived. Much of the book was written at their dining room table early in the morning. Mike and Brenda Sprott will always occupy a special place of love and respect in my heart.

*The Cup and the Glory* was written immediately after the wilderness ended from October through December in 1996. As it will be repeatedly shown, I did not know that I was writing a book; I was writing chapters of what I had learned in my studies. By no means did God inspire me, but I certainly did sense a divine compulsion—not so much to write, but to find holy, divine answers from God's holy, divine Word. Many nights, in spite of my best efforts, I could not sleep. Try as I might, even when taking my strongest pain medicine left in my little arthritis kit—it didn't matter: I stayed up.

Sometimes the study would be so intense I would start around 11:00 PM, study for a little while, look out my window, and much to my astonishment, see the sun rising. In other words, what seemed like an hour or so of study was actually 6-8 hours. I knew I was finding the answers to many of my questions from God's Word, and it just gripped me to do so. I was neither reluctant nor did I fight against it. It was the type of study that once I began, I never really came out of it (nor desired to come out) until it was complete. I did not do this study for anyone else; I was having my soul fed by the Lord, and He had created an insatiable hunger and thirst for Him and His Word.

Because my commitment in Charlotte took only two days of the week, and the early morning hours on Wednesdays were good writing time, God had permitted me the opportunity to devote myself to this study almost full-time, and I did so with gusto. I knew virtually nothing about what ended up in the book until God took me through chapter by chapter. I was so different by the time what became the book ended. Below is a synopsis, the rationale and the order for each chapter.

### First chapter written: Chapter Two—"The Cup"

"The Wilderness" ended exactly at the time God led me into the study of Mark 10:35-41. I have no idea to this day how I got to that passage other than by the Lord's leading. As I read these verses I could not think fast enough or write fast enough. This study became the foundation for "The Cup" chapter, and with a few additions added later, I wrote almost the entire chapter at one sitting. Instead of 1 Peter 5:10 (which was the verse that I did not believe would ever be true for me), Mark 10:35-41 was what I knew I was to preach when I went back to speak at Washington Bible College for my first time since I had resigned.

The Thursday night before I spoke in chapel at WBC, I went down to eat with Roland and De Lee. It was just like old times, only this time I wore shoes. De was still at work, so Roland and I had some quality time alone before she came home. I walked Roland through what God had taught me and what I would be speaking on in chapel the next day. He took his own notes as I went through the text. He kept saying excitedly, "Slow down! Slow down! There's so much in here!"—and he was right.

What a sweet blessing to be able to watch God minister to Roland much in the same way He had just ministered to me a few days before. I was able to witness my friend dear Roland, who only had less than three years left in his earthly walk, respond in worship to God much in the same way that I had: just abject, stunned amazement at God and His goodness, shaking his head slowly from side to side in silence as he mused on the Word. As I mentioned before, he was the first one to say, "You really need to write this down" (which I had begun to do). Some people paint (I wish I could); some sing; some do wood work or other things. Like some others, I write. I have always enjoyed doing so, and I just gravitated toward it (such as with the Twins' letter).

I left the Lee's apartment after supper and returned to my guest quarters at WBC in hope of getting a good night's sleep before I was to speak in chapel in the morning. However, during the early evening I started to get sick, and it became worse throughout the night. In the same hallway where I had previously been sick months before with a food poisoning and a high fever that doctors believe triggered the arthritis, I spent the entire night with a fever, repeatedly throwing up, lying on the floor (my old routine), and I had only a barely audible whisper of a voice once the sun came up.

Having just come out of "The Wilderness," I prayed that God would allow me to speak in chapel. I do not mean this as some sort of manly boast, but I had already settled in my mind that if I had to crawl there and be propped up that, if God so enabled, I intended to speak in chapel the next morning. I showered, having to sit down repeatedly in the shower because I could not stand, and got ready as best I could. Still being sick, I slowly headed to the service, pausing several times along the way to keep from passing out. I was hoping I could somehow make it through the preaching.

Of course, this is not exactly a flashy or impressive way of speaking to a group: sitting in a chair, sweat drenching my shirt and dripping from the tip of my nose onto my notes, speaking with a raspy voice, hoarse, barely audible without the microphone—such was how I did chapel that day. We went through "The Cup" section out of Mark 10:35-41. When I had finished I was quite astounded. Never in my years in the ministry had I witnessed such a massive response as I did after this message. After I finished, there was a reverential hush (almost silence) as people left the chapel. This was the first time I did a glory chapter or series in public, and I remember thinking to myself, "What I just did is real good or real bad—but it is not marginal." I spoke with some of those who had attended the chapel, both immediately after the message and later that day, and I knew what had happened was reverence before God and certainly not before me. I had never seen this with a group before, especially one that large.

I have thought about that chapel service often over the years. Looking back on it I think that God purposely showed me a small display of the power of His Word. The physical limitations no more hindered His Word from going forth than did Paul's thorn in the flesh. My weakness was made perfect in His strength; His strength was perfected in my weakness; His grace was more than sufficient.

I went back and finished writing "The Cup" chapter by editing it and by reading it to the group that I met with in Charlotte. What became chapter two of the book ("The Cup") was actually the first chapter I wrote. As I mentioned in the first chapter of the printed book, I never intended to write a book. "The Cup" was a chapter—isolated, not part of something bigger. I wanted to write it (which I did) because I was sure I would use it again elsewhere.

### Second chapter written: Chapter Three—"The Road"

"The Road" was from a Sunday School class I taught at a church in Wake Forest, NC. The class wanted me to do an introduction to the Book of Philippians, and I did so from Acts 16 because it tells how God directed Paul to Philippi. I was beginning to see God bring a much bigger picture into focus (especially the part that it was no mistake or bad misfortune that had happened to me and my family). Everything was connected. The Cup consists of a process that is part of our Christian walk; since there is a Christian walk, then obviously there must be a place to walk—hence the name "The Road."

This was the first place in which I saw my own experience laid out in Scripture in someone else's life. I had never noticed the repeated closed doors *by God* in Acts 16. The doors did not close by themselves; God closed the doors. It is easy to see this in other people's lives; it is different to view this in your own.

This chapter ministered to me greatly, even though it was so early in my studies on this. What a wonderful encouragement to be in such good company. The specific reference to each member of the Trinity in this chapter was very touching in that a loving God would leave such beautiful markers in His Word that He is indeed active and present, even when we do not perceive Him to be.

When the book was finally published, I was out of the country and had to wait ten days before I saw my first copy; yet what a blessed place to be. When I taught at Southeastern Baptist Seminary and college, I was asked to help with "The Footsteps of Paul" study tour. On four different occasions I was privileged to go to the cities where Paul planted churches (and to visit the other nearby sights of the churches of Revelation 2 and 3). So the day after the book came out in America, our study group was on the actual, physical "road to Troas" in Turkey. Most of the people on the bus had no idea of the significance of where we were. A married couple who are friends of mine, Brad and Jess Canelejo, whom I had in my classes numerous times, had a, ratty, beat-up unpublished copy of *The Cup and the Glory* with several spelling and grammatical errors. For years I would either print out copies of the book or send them via email to people who made requests for them. I would "charge them prayer" and tell them to pass copies on to those who they thought needed them. To this day I have no idea where all of the copies ended, but before publication I knew they had gone to at least seventy countries. Brad and Jess had brought along such a copy.

Looking back on those copies, they had so many mistakes; yet the core truths were there—and that is what ministers to people. What a privilege to teach a session about "the road to Troas" on the literal road to Troas. We could look out the bus window and see exactly where Paul was as he traveled. The old copy of the book also made the rounds as several people on the group read it during the trip.

### Third chapter written: Chapter Four—"The Gift"

Since "The Road" came from a study in Acts 16 that records how God directed Paul to Philippi and then what happened once he arrived, it reasons that Philippians would be a good place to continue the study. I had begun my studies with 1 Peter 5:10 in mind and was trying to get back there, but I knew "The Road" had deeply ministered to me. Although I knew I was headed back to 1 Peter, I by no means wanted to miss any of the goldmines God wanted me to see along the way. So before going to 1 Peter, I thought it appropriate to read through Philippians.

In reading the Book of Philippians, my life changed forever when I came to Philippians 1:29. I had a rheumatologist appointment on the other side of town. I had taken my Greek Bible and a legal pad to a restaurant in Raleigh so I could study before the appointment. When I read what this verse said in the Greek, I looked away from the text (as though looking away could somehow change the content of the Word). I slowly read it from the Greek text about six times in a row. "This verse *cannot* be saying what it says," I kept saying silently to myself. Yet it most certainly did: grace gifted by God for salvation we readily accept; grace gifted by God for suffering, we do not.

Some of you may know Isaiah 55:8-9: "'For My thoughts are not your thoughts, neither are your ways My ways,' declares the LORD. 'For as the heavens are higher than the earth, so are My ways higher than your ways, and My thoughts than your thoughts.'" Oh yeah? Give me an example. Philippians 1:29: "For to you it has been granted for Christ's sake, not only to believe in Him, but also to suffer for His sake." While I had read the Isaiah verses many times and had even referred to them often, I think this was the first time such a verse stopped me in my tracks. This teaching was so against my understanding of what would be considered a gift from God.

So "The Gift" chapter was researched and later written. As with the previous two chapters, while this is the fourth chapter in the book, it is actually the third one written (after "The Cup" and "The Road"). Also, I still had no concept that I was writing a book. I was writing chapters that were summaries of the different studies I was doing. I followed the trail in Scripture that was unfolding before me. I knew I was writing chapters; I just did not yet know that the chapters were indeed connected and would become part of the bigger project—namely, what ultimately materialized as the book.

### Fourth chapter written: Chapter Five—"The Counting" or "The Ledger"

Those of you who have read *The Cup and the Glory* may immediately notice that this chapter does not occur in the book. When I originally wrote this chapter, I was not sure of the title, and I went back and forth between the two listed above. The chapter initially was based on Philippians 3:7-8: "But whatever things were gain to me, those things I have counted as loss for the sake of Christ. More than that, I count all things to be loss in view of the surpassing value of knowing Christ Jesus my Lord, for whom I have suffered the loss of all things, and count them but rubbish in order that I may gain Christ." Hence, "The Counting" or "The Ledger" seemed to be an appropriate description.

It was not that the chapter was bad; it just did not fit with the others, and it was eventually removed from the book. More about this later under the writing of "The Fellowship" chapter.

### Fifth chapter written: Chapter Six—"The Footprints"

As I have repeatedly referenced, 1 Peter 5:10 (the "after you have suffered for a little while" verse) was where I originally started my study. I kept trying to get back there, but I kept being delayed by the goldmines I was finding. As with the writing of other chapters, I was in no hurry whatsoever to end this precious mining expedition.

I first studied this chapter while preaching through 1 Peter while I was serving as pastor at Berwyn Baptist Church in College Park, Maryland. The Word had so ministered to me in the preparation that week; it was a very worshipful time. I preached essentially what would later become "The Footprints" on a cold, rainy Sunday morning. The church's roof had sprung multiple leaks, and we had buckets strategically arranged to catch the raindrops. The attendance that morning was a little less than usual for some reason, but none of that mattered. We had gold that morning—worship-evoking gold—and I knew it to my core. How could we possibly have thought about the roof and some leaks when we started to understand what our Savior did for us, and how He alone was able to do what no one else could do?

Two things make this chapter different from the others. First, "The Footprints" was the first chapter that was based on verses from 1 Peter. In fact, "The Footprints," "The Surprise," "The Blessing" and "The Agreement" all originate from this beloved epistle and appear in order. For example, "The Footprints" was from 1 Peter 2:21-25, and "The Surprise" was from 1 Peter 4, etc.

The second item that made this chapter different was that this was the first time I ever saw how substantial the connection was between what Peter wrote decades later in his epistle and what Jesus taught him and others in the Gospels. Nothing just happened with the writing of 1 Peter (or with other books either). God sovereignly led and developed the vessel He would use to bring about His inspired Word.

From this chapter through the present time, I always go back and see if there is any relevance with what Jesus taught in the Gospels to those who would later become the biblical writers, especially Peter and John. Time after time Jesus taught Peter (and others) truths that never left him. So often even the exact wording, Scripture references, phrases or sentences are used. I have not reached the bottom of this goldmine; the studies only get better.

### Sixth chapter written: Chapter Seven—"The Surprise"

Still on my way back to 1 Peter 5:10, I had to stop at verses which intrigued and convicted me. First Peter 4:12-13 state, "Beloved, do not be surprised at the fiery ordeal among you, which comes upon you for your testing, as though some strange thing were happening to you; but to the degree that you share the sufferings of Christ, keep on rejoicing; so that also at the revelation of His glory, you may rejoice with exultation." *Everything* in this verse properly described what I had previously thought, murmured, complained and prayed about over the years—not on a constant level, but with peaks and valleys. "Do not be surprised"—I was surprised. "Fiery ordeal"—yes, it was. "As though some strange thing were happening to you"—I thought it was a strange thing, very strange.

It is funny how you can read some verses like these over and over only to have parts of them that you have skimmed over suddenly stop you in your tracks. That is what happened with these verses. I had completely missed that explanation from God that the fiery ordeal "comes upon you for your testing." This changed my perspective. I think many of us consider that such testing is reserved for Job or especially for Jesus. Yet here were first century Christians—men, women and children, most of whom we have no idea of their names—who were greatly tested in their walk with God.

This made me evaluate and certainly start to look differently at the past three-and-a-half years of my life. Previously I had seen only the events; I did not have the spiritual perspective to see the bigger picture. These testings were related; these testings were purposeful on God's part. All that had occurred was part of the composite of what *God* was doing—not that the testings were done in the absence of God's presence. In fact, God used Roland Lee to start adjusting my perspective, when in the midst of "The Wilderness" Roland told me, "You know, this is something God trusts you with." I had not thought of it in those terms before, and what Roland said was in essence the teaching of 1 Peter 4:12-13.

We often miss another key component of these verses: this type of testing has to be to such a degree that it causes us to be surprised; otherwise, there would be no need for the "Beloved, do not be surprised" command by Peter. As it is written in the book, I was surprised. I was surprised at how hard, how deep, how long, how seemingly endless—and on it goes. I have found that to be the case with many other believers across the globe.

**Seventh chapter written: Chapter Eight—"The Blessing"**

I was still on my way to 1 Peter 5:10. First Peter 4:14 was a place I knew I had to stop and explore: "If you are reviled for the name of Christ, you are blessed, because the Spirit of glory and of God rests upon you." What really struck me in this chapter was more the present aspect of this "you are blessed" rather than the future tense "you will be blessed" as part of your eternal reward from God. Also, in spite of our struggling and often stumbling along (from our own vantage point), for those who submit to God, He promises: "the Spirit of glory and of God rests upon you." Of course, that is God's explanation for what comprises the blessing (at least in the present verse). Our vantage point focuses on the severity of the testing; God focuses on the testing that leads to a specific purpose He desires.

I saw how vastly different my assessment of blessing was from God's assessment. It is a most humbling process to do this, but it was absolutely necessary for God patiently to teach me in the many, many areas where I came up short. God was already changing me eternally by my feeding on His Word. I was also getting used to the idea of discovery in the Bible that showed how far off-base many of my assessments were about my life and what had happened. I was beginning to see how many good promises from God originate out of what we consider hard and horrible events in our lives. In reality, this was just an ongoing process of acknowledging that His thoughts are not my thoughts and His ways are not my ways—but I was lovingly being spiritually healed by the Good Shepherd in a way that only He and His Word can do.

**Eighth chapter written: Chapter One—"The Wilderness"**

I had written seven chapters by this time. I sometimes think people do not fully believe me when I tell them this, but I had no idea I was writing a book until about this time. I was writing chapters of my studies. I knew I would use these again either in the classroom or in a church setting. I had no intention of throwing these away, but I had no design or scheme which I was following. The chapters were isolated and independent.

Then as I was beginning to understand a little more of the mind of God in such matters, I felt the necessity to go back and look from a new perspective not only at what had happened in my life, but also at what I had found in my studies. Since the previous chapter had said, "Do not be surprised at the fiery ordeal among you that comes upon you for your testing," I thought it appropriate to write a brief description of aspects of my particular fiery trial.

I am one of those "heart on the table" or "what you see is what you get" guys, so I had to write the chapter this way. The only way I knew how to do this accurately was to write it as if I were telling a friend what it was like, exposing my own weakness, frustrations and failures. The death of our Twins had been a part; the arthritis had been a part; the road to Troas had been a part as well, although I didn't know what to call it at the time.

One thing that describes the wilderness is the complete lack of direction (from our perspective) that surrounds us when we are within its midst. It would be so much easier to walk from Point A to Point B, if we knew where Point B was. But in the wilderness we have no direction whatsoever. I tried to describe the wilderness as best I could, remembering what it was like. I was no longer there; I wrote it after the fact and on the outside looking in. I was much more along the road by that time. But when I was in the wilderness I did not know what it was, why it was or how long it would last. My sinful assumption was that it would never end—but it did. Looking back on it, I am so glad God brought me into the wilderness and through it. *Everything* about it was necessary for God to accomplish His will in my life—and in anyone else's life who goes through this same desolate training ground.

### Tenth chapter written: Chapter Nine—"The Agreement"

Well, I finally had made it back to the verse I originally started with, but it had been some rich and blessed study getting there. How appropriate that even though I thought, "I finally get to dig into 1 Peter 5:10," the word "and" (or "but") in 5:10 showed the connection to the immediate context. In spite of my multiple readings of this verse, I had never noticed this before. It was almost like there was a divine cough "Ahem!" as in, "There is more connected to this verse." So actually I worked my way backward and saw the perfect, holy logic of God's teaching. I still was, in a sense, examining Him, while the previous verses call us to examine our own walk. Looking back, I had only sporadically done what 1 Peter 5:5-9 commands us to do. I was expecting God to work; He was patiently waiting for me to do what His Word commanded me—not suggested to me.

This was the first chapter that I wrote knowing that it would actually be part of a book. Thus the tone of the book changed from my writing primarily to myself alone (and with Roland in mind) and knowing that this would be for others as well. I had and still have no idea whom God intended this book for; we will see what God does as He unfolds it. Since I started writing with others in mind, you will find the repeated phrase, "Stand firm" used throughout this chapter as the same exhortation that Peter/the Holy Spirit gave in 1 Peter.

I had very few people to talk with when I wrote this. At the time I kept wondering and asking myself, "I wonder if anyone else doesn't know this?" Or, "I wonder if anyone else has struggled with these same questions?" Many times by this point I also pondered, "I wonder if anyone else will be ministered to by what God's Word teaches in the same manner that I had been?" It is different now since I have found out in the testimonies of thousands that it is much more common than I thought. I just had no idea as I wrote many of the chapters at the Sprott residence in Charlotte in the predawn hours.

### Tenth chapter written: Chapter Ten—"The Glory"

So now what? I had made it back to my original verse of 1 Peter 5:10. I had learned and had been fed by God so much during this time. I knew I had written a book; I had no idea at the time what exactly I had written. I had no idea of the title. After all, how can you entitle a book for which you cannot describe what it contained? So I went back and read what I had written, hoping to find some continuity or theme. Since the first chapter written was "The Cup," putting "The Cup" in the title made sense. Because James and John's request in Mark 10 was made in reference to sitting in the glory of Jesus, that made sense as well. And, as you know, Jesus' answer about sitting in His glory goes back to being able to drink the cup that He—and others—must drink. As I read the chapters and the related Scriptures, the repeated couplets of "suffering and glory" were found. Hence, the title became obvious: *The Cup and the Glory.*

So I started this final chapter in a different way: I had a title for the chapter before I had even a word of the contents. Because I had taken the title from the request of James and John, it reasoned that the events related to that would be a good place to start following the trail in Scripture to see where it would lead. Yet, as was fitting, I had absolutely no idea what I was going to write or even if there would be a trail to follow. This was not like some of the chapters before where I had taught them in a class setting or in preaching through 1 Peter. I prayed that God would lead me through this one as well. I was hesitant in thinking that I might have nine chapters but would not have an appropriate concluding chapter. As I began this study I actually naively thought to myself, "I sure hope there's enough information in here to get a chapter out of this." Oh, foolish man and slow of heart to believe!

As I started my study for this concluding chapter, I did not want to hurry through it or "finally get this over with." I had no sense of finishing a race or accomplishing a project. Instead, there was a sense of pause and repose and enjoyment of God before beginning this final segment. God had patiently and lovingly taught me so much by the time I got here. I sensed that the previous chapters written were large plateau steps, and we rested on this one, savoring the moment before making the final ascent.

### Eleventh chapter written: Chapter Five—"The Fellowship"

When I finished *The Cup and the Glory,* I knew that God had wonderfully ministered to me through His Word. The Good Shepherd had indeed Himself perfected, confirmed, strengthened and established me (1 Peter 5:10). Yet even after the book was written, I also knew something was not quite right about it; however, I could not figure out what it was. It continually gnawed at me for a couple of weeks, as I almost continually pondered throughout the day what was lacking.

Something about it just was not right. For lack of better description, it was similar to an annoying popcorn hull that I could not remove wedged firmly in my teeth. Finally, it dawned on me that the problem was the fifth chapter. Those of you who have read the book know that the fifth chapter is entitled "The Fellowship." That, however, was not its original name or content.

Initially the chapter title was either going to be "The Counting" or "The Ledger," taken from Philippians 3:7-8: "But whatever things were gain to me, those things I have counted as loss for the sake of Christ. More than that, I count all things to be loss in view of the surpassing value of knowing Christ Jesus my Lord, for whom I have suffered the loss of all things, and count them but rubbish in order that I may gain Christ." Paul employed accountants' terminology in these verses: on one side of the ledger is the loss column; on the other side is the gain. Paul's counting in his ledger regarded the loss of all things; but even more so, he immeasurably gained the Lord Jesus Christ.

So I knew the problem was with the fifth chapter, but I still did not know what was wrong with it. It is one thing to know that something is not right; it is quite another to know how to correct it. After I went back and read through it, I understood that the biggest reason this chapter did not fit was that it would have placed the emphasis on *me* counting the cost and *me* suffering loss (and gain). Philippians 3:10 is much more appropriate for the overall flow and focus of the book: "that I may know Him, and the power of His resurrection and the fellowship of His sufferings, being conformed to His death." Hence, a change in the title occurred, namely then becoming "The Fellowship."

Even more so the content was completely changed. Simply put, "The Fellowship" is about His suffering—not ours. When we even remotely understand what this verse teaches, we more vastly appreciate what Jesus endured for us. We compare His suffering with how small ours is/was, and it humiliates us into worshipful adoration of Him. Knowing that we fail and struggle and often whine in the midst of our trials makes Jesus' response stand so much in contrast to ours. Yet even beyond this, His sufferings vastly exceeded more than we will ever begin to conceive in our minds until we are home with the Lord.

I sat down and wrote this chapter pretty much straight through at one sitting. I actually dreaded doing so because I knew the only way I could write it was to step back into the circle of grief. I went upstairs to my home office in Wake Forest and wept through every word of this chapter, often stopping to thank God in prayer and praise for His suffering in my behalf.

So "The Fellowship" chapter has three unique features. First, it became the only chapter of the book that was completely rewritten from beginning to end. Second, although it is found in the middle of the book, it actually was the last chapter written. I think even its placement in the book is perfect: at the midpoint of the study, the focus goes back to Jesus and what He accomplished for the redeemed.

One final aspect about this chapter emerged years later. It had always been there; I just did not realize it. The third and final unique feature about "The Fellowship" is that it became the springboard and connection with *The Darkness and the Glory*. More about that later.

Also available from **Kress Christian**
PUBLICATIONS

*Christian Living Beyond Belief: Biblical Principles for the Life of Faith*
Cliff McManis

*One with a Shepherd: The Tears and Triumphs of a Ministry Marriage*
Mary Somerville

*Meeting God Behind Enemy Lines: My Christian Testimony as a U.S. Navy SEAL*
Steve Watkins

*God's Plan for Israel: A Study of Romans 9-11*
Steve Kreloff

*God in Everyday Life: The Book of Ruth for Expositors and Biblical Counselors*
Brad Brandt & Eric Kress

*Free Justification: The Glorification of Christ in the Justification of a Sinner*
Steve Fernandez

*Commentaries for Biblical Expositors*
Dr. Jim Rosscup

*Revelation 20 and the Millennial Debate*
Matt Waymeyer

*A Biblical Critique of Infant Baptism*
Matt Waymeyer

*Notes for the Study and Exposition of 1st John*
Eric Kress

The Gromacki Expository Series (by Dr. Robert Gromacki)
*Called to Be Saints: An Exposition of 1 Corinthians*
*Stand Firm in the Faith: An Exposition of 2 Corinthians*
*Stand Fast in Liberty: An Exposition of Galatians*
*Stand United in Joy: An Exposition of Philippians*
*Stand Perfect in Wisdom: An Exposition of Colossians & Philemon*
*Stand True to the Charge: An Exposition of 1 Timothy*
*Stand Bold in Grace: An Exposition of Hebrews*